Student Handbook

Jean–Claude Larréché

The Alfred H. Heineken Chaired Professor of Marketing

INSEAD

Hubert Gatignon

The Claude Janssen Chaired Professor of Business Administration
and Professor of Marketing

INSEAD

Rémi Triolet

Partner, Director of R&D

STRATX International

Publisher: STRATX International

Production: Coptech, Inc., Woburn, Massachusetts

Cover Design: Synergy Network, Waltham, Massachusetts

Marketing Team – Americas: Paul Ritmo, Andrea Hernandez

Marketing Team – Europe, Middle-East, Asia, Africa: Sabine Fabbricatore,
Patricia Huber

Development Team – Rémi Triolet, Didier Drobecq, Aurélien Dauvergne,
Christophe Pottier

ISBN# 0-9743063-0-4

Reprint 2008

Contents

Table of Illustrations

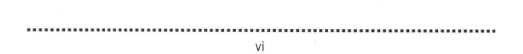

Introduction

Markstrat Online is the latest version of the MARKSTRAT simulation. The original MARKSTRAT simulation was developed more than twenty years ago by Jean-Claude Larréché, Alfred H. Heineken Professor of Marketing at INSEAD, and Hubert Gatignon, The Claude Janssen Chaired Professor of Business Administration and Professor of Marketing at INSEAD. Used in combination with traditional training methods such as conceptual sessions or case studies, Markstrat Online is a highly effective tool to learn strategic marketing concepts, such as brand portfolio strategy or segmentation and positioning strategy, as well as operational marketing. Similar to a flight simulator, this marketing simulation allows students and managers to practice new skills in an intensive time frame and in a risk-free environment before trying them out in their real business environment.

The mathematical model of MARKSTRAT, MARKSTRAT3 and Markstrat Online is based on solid theoretical foundations, and the underlying formulas have been extensively tested. These simulations have been used to successfully train a large number of students and executives from many universities and organizations.

You and your team will be given a company and product portfolio to manage in a dynamic and interactive environment. No previous computer experience is required but it is important to prepare by reading this handbook prior to beginning your course. If you do not read it carefully, you will run the risk of putting your team at a competitive disadvantage!

Questions & Technical Support

We have done our best to make this manual as clear and complete as possible. But the Markstrat Online simulation is fairly complex and we know by experience that some topics will require additional explanation. If you have questions regarding this handbook or the simulation we suggest that you follow the steps below.

Check the Online Help section of your Markstrat Online Team Software, in order to research General Information or view the FAQ section. Other students may have already asked a similar question, and a response may be available in the FAQs. Save time by checking the site first.

If you do not find the response to your question in the FAQs, please contact your instructor. Do not contact STRATX directly as we are not equipped to handle requests from thousands of students.

Responses to frequently asked questions do not address specific team situations and do not provide advice or hints on strategy, management, marketing, finances or any other topic. For these subjects, you should only count on your brains (or those of your teammates ...) and your experience.

Here are some examples of questions already addressed in the FAQs:

- What is the formula for the Stock Price Index?
- How are default decisions calculated?
- Is Markstrat Online compatible with Windows XP?
- Can you explain the position of circles on the growth-share matrix?
- Etc ...

X

About STRATX

STRATX is a unique training and development group that brings together disciplines from leading business schools, management consultants and learning design specialists. Founded by INSEAD Marketing Professor, Jean-Claude Larréché, our aim is to help managers boost performance by developing market-focused strategies and turning them into action. Moreover, our approach mobilizes a group of individuals behind a common goal with a common language to achieve results.

Our methodology is based on our belief that new skills must be learned through action and experience rather than from books or lectures. STRATX offers training solutions that include advanced business simulations, interactive concept discussions, team project work and a host of other traditional and online learning opportunities.

Over the past sixteen years, our R&D team has designed and developed a portfolio of world-class business simulations, including MARKSTRAT3, used in over 500 business schools, or e-Strat, used in the L'Oréal E-Strat Challenge since 1999.

With offices in Europe, North America and Asia, STRATX consultants design and deliver market leadership seminars for clients such as General Electric, Pfizer, Exxon, Hewlett-Packard, Novartis and Boeing.

1. Registration and Software Setup

You will have to go through a number of administrative steps before you are able to make your first set of decisions with Markstrat Online. Please read carefully the following pages as it is important that you perform these steps in the appropriate order and at the right time.

The tasks to perform are listed below and are explained in more detail in the following pages.

- Purchasing your own copy of this handbook and registering on our web site;

- Downloading and installing the Markstrat Online team software;

- Testing your installation and discovering the Markstrat environment with the PRACTICE industry.

1.1 The Registration Process

Why register

The usage of Markstrat Online is strictly reserved to registered students. The registration process will allow you to be uniquely identified in the Markstrat Online remote database. The username and password that you have chosen at registration will authenticate you when using the Markstrat Online software.

Registration is absolutely mandatory, for several reasons.

- As explained in chapter you will have to exchange data back and forth with your instructor during your Markstrat Online course. All data exchange will take place over the Internet, through a remote database server. For obvious security reasons, you will have to be fully authenticated before you are allowed to transfer data to or from the remote server.

- The Markstrat Online web site includes a Course Management facility, dedicated to professors. Using this facility, your professor can easily send emails to all registered students, to keep you informed of the latest course news (when will the next decision round start or finish, how the latest results look like, how to better perform in the Vodite market, ...). If you are not a registered user, you will not receive these emails and you might miss some important information.

How to register

The first step is to buy your own copy of this handbook. The license is only valid for the course you already registered for and cannot be used for any other course. The original username and password are valid for 1 year. The hardcopy of this handbook includes a sealed envelope with your personal *Markstrat Online ID Card* – Example only (see Figure 1).

KEEP YOUR PERSONAL MARKSTRAT ONLINE ID CARD IN A SAFE PLACE.

Front   Back

Figure 1 – Sample Markstrat Online ID card

The license number printed on the front of the card is unique. It is required to register on the Markstrat Online web site. If you purchased an e-copy of this handbook you will receive the unique license number either from your professor or via email.

The second step is to visit www.markstratonline.com, to select the *Registration* section and follow the instructions carefully. You will be asked to choose a username, password and to enter your course ID and your license number. The license number is printed on your ID Card and the Course ID should be given to you by your instructor. If you do not yet know your course ID, leave the cell blank and continue; you will be allowed to enter it later.

A MARKSTRAT course will usually last several weeks, the best way to remember all of this information is to write them down on the back of the ID Card, as shown on the sample card in Figure 1. The additional fields; *Industry ID, Team ID* and *Team Password* will be explained in chapter 2.

1.2 Downloading and Installing the Team Software

How to download the setup file

To download the software, visit our web site at http://www.markstratonline.com, type in your username and password in the *Login* section dedicated to registered users, and select *Downloads*. You will find a series of hyperlinks to download the manual, to download the setup file and to browse Frequently Asked Questions.

Click one of these links to initiate the download. Your browser may ask you whether you want to execute the file transfer directly from the site or save it to disk. Select the save to disk option and save the file on your local hard drive.

Computer Requirements

The <u>minimum</u> computer configuration required to operate the Markstrat Online software is the following:

- Pentium-based processor with 16 megabytes of memory;

- Hard disk with at least 20 megabytes of available storage;

- Internet connection (only during authentication and file transfers);

- Windows 95, 98, Millennium, 2000, NT4 or XP.

- Internet Explorer 5.0 and above.

Installing the Software

You should now have on your hard drive a self-installable setup file named *Markstrat-Online-Team-Setup-VXX.exe*. Double-click on this file to start the

setup procedure. A window entitled *Welcome to the InstallShield Wizard for Markstrat Online* pops up. Click on the Next button to continue the setup procedure.

A window pops up allowing you specify in which folder Markstrat Online should be installed. The default folder is shown on the right. We

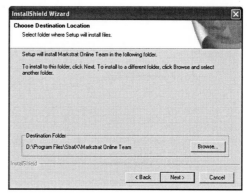

strongly advise you to use this default folder as it will make your life easier and reduce the risk of errors. For instance, reading the FAQs will be simplified as we will always refer to the default installation folder. If you need to install Markstrat Online in another folder, click on the *Browse...* button.

The actual installation starts when you click on the *Next >* button. All files are copied into the folder which you specified. Two of these files are registered automatically in the Windows registry.

The setup utility creates a shortcut called *Markstrat Online Team* on your desktop. Double-click on this shortcut to launch the application.

1.3 The PRACTICE Industry

You can now test your installation as well as your knowledge of the MARKSTRAT environment. All registered users can download a sample data file called PRACTICE. Refer to chapter 2.2 for these download instructions. The PRACTICE file is an actual data file, obtained during a past Markstrat Online course. You will be allowed to browse through all charts and graphs and to make decisions. However, you will not be able to check the results of your decisions as the PRACTICE file will not be run through the MARKSTRAT mathematical model.

2. The Interface Menu

The overall structure of the Markstrat Online team software is described in section 6.3 of this manual. This chapter focuses on the *Interface* menu, which is related to the administration of the course, i.e. to the communications that will take place between you, your teammates and the Instructor.

During your course, you will go through a number of *decision rounds*, usually 6 to 12 rounds. A decision round starts when you receive the latest simulation results, and it finishes when you submit a new set of decisions to the Instructor. The typical duration of a decision round is from 2 to 4 hours, depending on the time you are ready to devote to your MARKSTRAT exercise, or depending on constraints set by your instructor.

You and your teammates will have to decide on how to organize your work. The Markstrat Online software includes features to handle many possible situations. Here are a number of questions that will help you find the best possible organization.

- Will you work non-stop on your MARKSTRAT exercise for 3 hours from start to finish? Or will you spread your work over several days?

- Will all team members meet when they make decisions? Or are you geographically dispersed?

- Will all team members make decisions all together? Or will you assign responsibilities (R&D? Production, Finances ...) to team members, each making decisions on his or her own?

- Will you always work on the same computer? Or will you share your time between a computer in the University lab and your home computer?

- Will you always have a good internet connection? Or will you have to work on your MARKSTRAT exercise while being on the road?

In future sections, we will explain how to handle these different situations, and we will then explain various organization strategies.

2.1 Markstrat Online Overview

Figure 2 shows an overview of the Markstrat Online structure. All teams must exchange data back and forth with the instructor during the course. All data exchange will take place over the Internet, through a remote database server, called the Markstrat Online server. For security reasons, you will have to be fully authenticated before you are allowed to transfer data to or from the remote server.

The data to be exchanged are the simulation results and the teams' decisions. This data is located in a file called *team data file* or simply *team file*. There is only one file per team as all members of the same team share the same results and the same decisions. However, you will see that the team file can be duplicated on several computers if two or more teammates want to work in parallel.

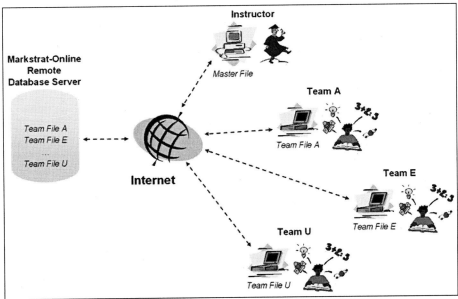

Figure 2 – Markstrat Online overview

Your instructor is in charge of putting your team file onto the Markstrat Online server at the beginning each decision round, so that you have access to the latest simulation results. The instructor is also responsible for taking your team file back from the Markstrat Online server, at the end of the decision round. This operation must be done just before running the simulation model, to produce a new set of results.

In between these two instructor's operations, you and your teammates are in charge of your team file. You will see in the next section that the team file can be downloaded from or uploaded to the Markstrat Online server; saved on your hard drive, on your LAN or on a removable storage (zip drive, disk, tape, flash USB drive, …) and duplicated on several computers.

2.2 Opening a Markstrat Online Session

A decision round is composed of one or several working sessions with the Markstrat Online software. You could make a detailed analysis of your results on day 1, make R&D and brand portfolio decisions on day 2, make marketing mix decisions on day 3 and finalize everything on the day 4.

The Markstrat Online software includes an Open Session assistant to guide you through the beginning of your working session. As this assistant is easy to use and self-explainable, we only discuss the most important steps here.

Which team file to use

Select Open session in the Interface menu to initiate the session. The window shown in Figure 3 pops up. Three choices are available.

- **_Download the PRACTICE file from the Markstrat Online server._** Select this option if you want to test your installation or to discover the MARKSTRAT environment. All registered users can download a sample data file called PRACTICE, obtained during a past Markstrat Online course. You will be allowed to browse through all charts and graphs and to make decisions. However, you will not be able to check the results of your decisions as the PRACTICE file cannot be run through the MARKSTRAT mathematical model

- **_Download your team file from the Markstrat Online server._** You need to download your team file from the Markstrat Online server at the beginning of each decision round. The file you will receive will contain the most recent simulation results, provided by your instructor. You also need to download the file if you or one of your teammates has already downloaded the file, made some decisions and uploaded the file back to the server. Your team file is named INDUSTRY-TEAMX.zip where INDUSTRY is the name of your industry (A,E,I,O,U or Y). The file is located in the folder "My Markstrat Online files" in your "My documents" main folder.

- **_Open a team file located on your hard drive, on your LAN or on a removable storage._** With this option, you will be able to open a team file that was saved _locally_, at the end of a previous working session. Indeed, when you close your session, your team file is saved automatically on your hard-drive but you also have the choice to upload it back to the Markstrat

Online server, and/or to save a copy on another local resource, for example; LAN or removable storage.

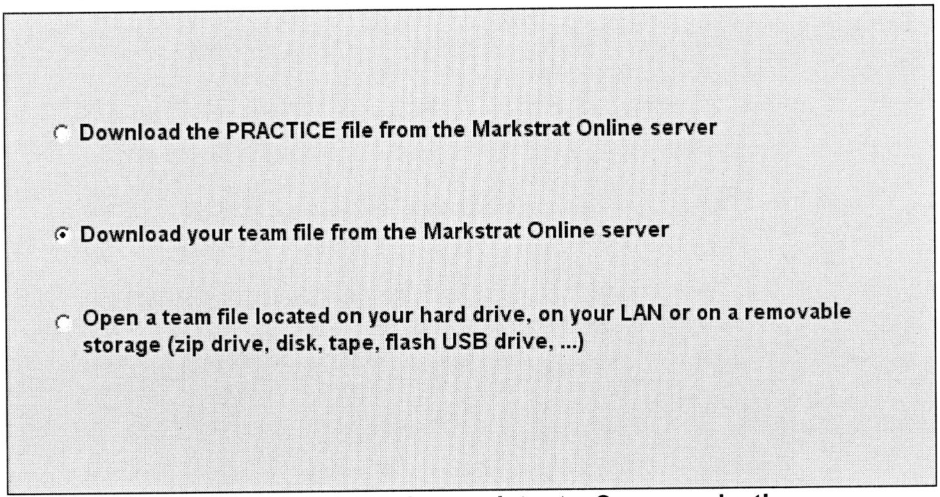

  ◯ Download the PRACTICE file from the Markstrat Online server

  ⦿ Download your team file from the Markstrat Online server

  ◯ Open a team file located on your hard drive, on your LAN or on a removable
    storage (zip drive, disk, tape, flash USB drive, ...)

Figure 3 – Open session assistant – Source selection

Authentication

This step is required each time you connect to the Markstrat Online server, either to download or to upload your team file. For security reasons, access to the Markstrat Online server is reserved to registered students. If you are not yet registered, please refer to section 1.1 of this manual.

The window shown in Figure 4 pops up. Enter the username and password that you choose upon registration and select *Next*. The software will connect to the Markstrat Online remote database server and check your identification. Please, note that you must be connected to internet before trying to authenticate.

If you do not remember your password, you can go to our web site www.markstratonline.com and in the *Student Login* section, a special page is devoted to lost usernames and/or passwords; with the license number printed on your Markstrat Online ID Card, you will be able to retrieve your personal data.

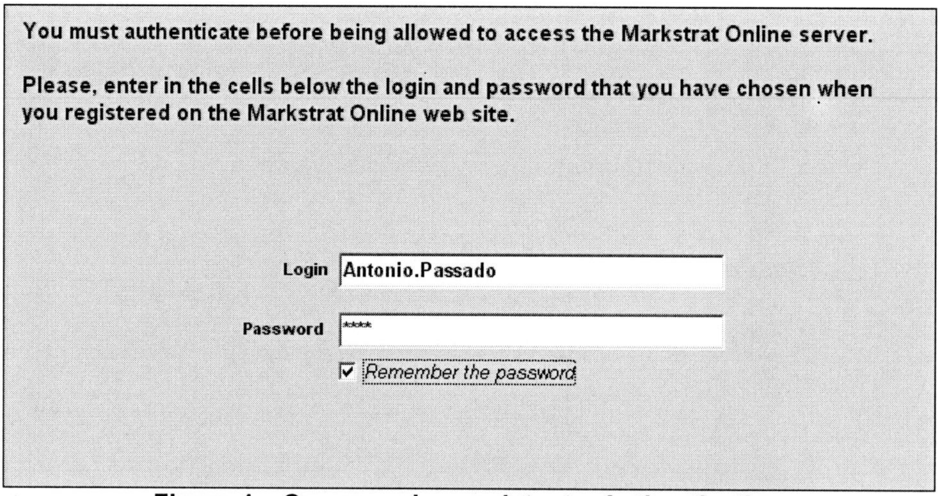

You must authenticate before being allowed to access the Markstrat Online server.

Please, enter in the cells below the login and password that you have chosen when you registered on the Markstrat Online web site.

Login Antonio.Passado

Password ****

☑ *Remember the password*

Figure 4 – Open session assistant – Authentication

If you are working on your own computer, you can check the option *Remember the password*. Your password will be stored locally and you will no longer have to key it in. Beware; *this option should not be used on shared computers.*

Industry and Team Selection

This step is required to download your team file from the Markstrat Online server. You must indicate your industry ID, your team ID and, for confidentiality reasons, your team password. Type your ID's and password in the window shown in Figure 5 and select *Next*.

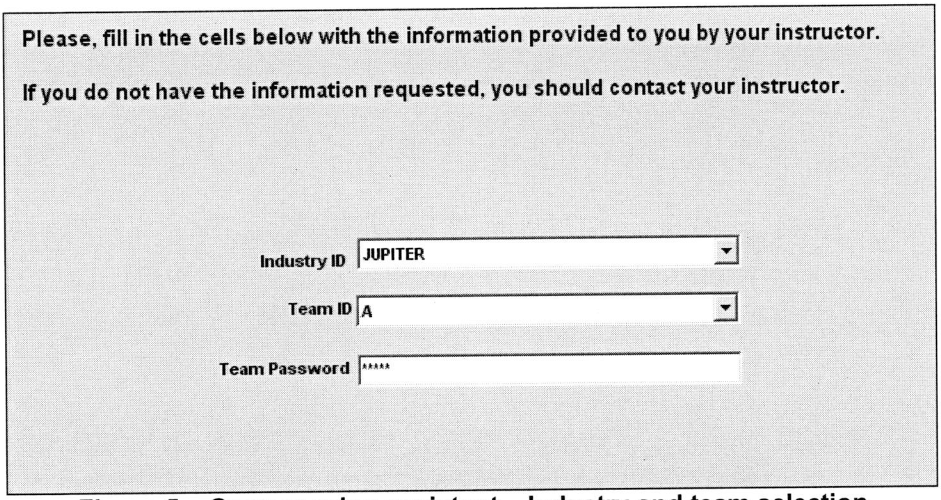

Industry ID JUPITER

Team ID A

Team Password *****

Figure 5 – Open session assistant – Industry and team selection

These three pieces of information will be given to you by your instructor, most likely during class or by email. Please, write them down on your Markstrat Online ID CARD, as shown on Figure 1.

2.3 Closing a Markstrat Online Session

The Markstrat Online software includes a *Close Session* assistant to guide you through the end of your working session. As this assistant is easy to use and self-explainable, we only discuss the most important steps here.

Saving your team file

Your industry file is saved automatically each time you modify your decisions and click OK. Thus, you can interrupt your work at any time and restart it without being connected to the Internet. All you have to do is select the third option of Figure 3 and reopen your team file.

Closing your session

Select *Close session* in the *Interface* menu to finish the session. The window shown in Figure 6 pops up. Two options are available; they can be both activated at the same time.

- **Upload your team file to the Markstrat Online server.** You should upload your team file each time you modify your decisions so that your teammates, your instructor or yourself can retrieve the file later. If you are not connected to internet, you can save a copy of the file locally, open it later and upload it when you have a connection.

- **Save a copy of your team file on your hard drive, on your LAN or on a removable storage.** This option is useful in several situations. For instance, if you want to move your team file onto a computer not connected to internet. In this case, you can save a copy of your team file on a removable storage (zip drive, disk, tape, flash USB drive ...) and then use this storage on another computer.

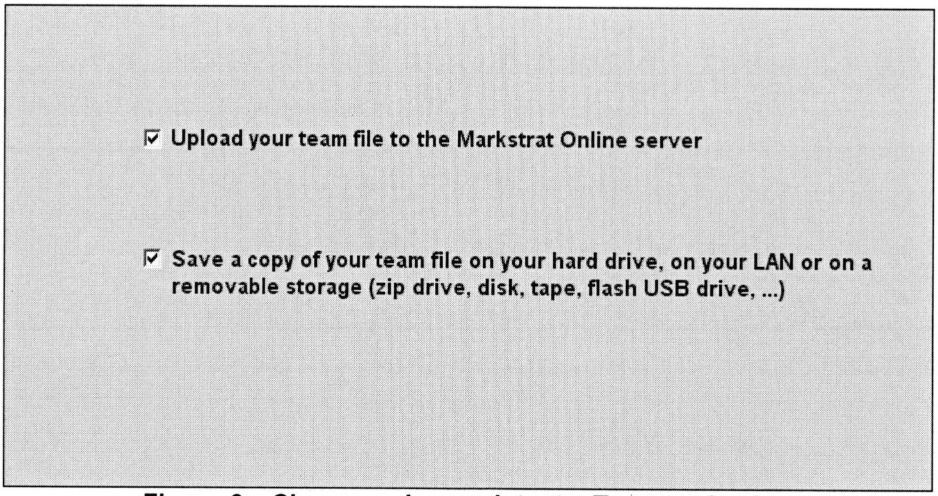

☑ **Upload your team file to the Markstrat Online server**

☑ **Save a copy of your team file on your hard drive, on your LAN or on a removable storage (zip drive, disk, tape, flash USB drive, ...)**

Figure 6 – Close session assistant – Target selection

Note that if you select only the second option, *your team file will not be saved* on the Markstrat Online server.

Authentication

The authentication step is mandatory only if you select the first option, i.e. if you upload your team file to the Markstrat Online server. Refer to page 11 for more info on the authentication step.

3. Overview of the MARKSTRAT World

3.1 Your Role

You and the other members of your team have just been recruited by a large corporation to manage the marketing department of one of its divisions. Coming from a different industry, your team has no experience of the MARKSTRAT world. In the coming years, you will compete with several other firms to market two types of durable goods to consumers. During this exercise, you will be responsible for formulating and implementing the long-term marketing strategy of your division. In particular, you and your team members will have to:

- target selected segments and position your products in a highly competitive market;

- interface with the R&D department to design and develop new products;

- prepare the launch of new products, improve, maintain or withdraw existing ones;

- interface with the Production department to specify production planning;

- make marketing mix decisions, such as pricing or advertising budget, for each brand in your portfolio;

- decide on the size and priorities of your sales force;

- order market research studies that provide up-to-date information for decision making.

3.2 Overview of the MARKSTRAT World

The MARKSTRAT world is a fictitious industrialized country of 250 million inhabitants whose monetary unit is the MARKSTRAT dollar ($). In this country both inflation and GNP growth are fairly stable, and no major political, social or economic event is anticipated in the near future. The MARKSTRAT world does not intend to represent any particular country, market or industrial sector. However, it roughly behaves like most markets, and the general management and marketing knowledge that you have acquired through business experience or formal education applies to this new world.

In the MARKSTRAT world, there are a handful of competing companies that manufacture and market consumer durable goods. These goods are comparable to electronic products such as hi-fi systems, telephone sets or computers as well as office equipment, cars, books, or any other consumer durable goods. With most scenarios, each firm starts in a different situation in terms of product specification, target customer groups, brand awareness levels, market share, distribution coverage, profitability, R&D expertise, etc. Consequently, the marketing strategy of each firm should be adapted to its particular situation within the industry. However, Markstrat Online includes a few scenarios where all firms start in the exact same situation. These scenarios are called *competition* scenario and your instructor will let you know if you are using them.

Nevertheless, no firm has a relative advantage over the others and initially many characteristics are common to all firms. For instance, the initial brand portfolio of all companies is comprised of two brands. As mentioned before, each firm will have the opportunity to design and develop new R&D projects and to introduce new products or upgrade existing ones. All R&D departments have the same capabilities to develop new projects, in their range of experience. Similarly, all sales forces are equally qualified to handle distributor relationships.

3.3 Sonite Products

At the beginning of the simulation, all rival firms market two *Sonite* brands. Sonite products have existed for several years and the market has grown quite consistently since the introduction of the first Sonite brand. It is now a well-established market, with several strong brands at different price points covering a wide range of needs. Analysts believe that the Sonite market will continue to grow over the next five years.

A Sonite is a complex piece of equipment made up of several components. Although they can be evaluated along more than fifty attributes, Sonite brands are primarily differentiated in terms of the five most important physical characteristics listed in Figure 7. The *base cost* is also an important parameter; this is the cost at which each unit will be produced, based on an initial production batch of 100,000 units. The base cost is decided jointly by the Marketing department -which is mainly concerned by margin and profitability- and by the R&D department -which is mainly concerned with product feasibility. Only the following characteristics will be considered during the course of the simulation:

Characteristic	Unit	Feasible range
Weight	Kilogram (kg)	10 – 20
Design	Index	3 – 10
Volume	Cubic decimeter (dm³)	20 – 100
Maximum frequency (refers to the band width)	Kilohertz (kHz)	5 – 50
Power	Watt (W)	5 – 100
Base cost	$	10 +

Figure 7 – Sonite main physical characteristics

Note that design is not related to the product esthetic but to the type of raw materials used (wood, plastic, metal ...) or to the aspect of its various components. Therefore, a product rated 8 on the design scale is not better or easier-to-use than one rated 4 on the same scale.

All brands marketed in a given period will be listed in the corresponding Newsletter, in a table similar to Figure 8.

3.4 Vodite Products

Recently, there has been industry speculation that a new type of electronic product might emerge, the *Vodite*. Although no Vodite brands are available at the start of the simulation, industry experts have a pretty good idea of what future Vodite products might resemble.

Vodite products will satisfy entirely different needs from that of Sonite products so that demand for the two products will be completely independent. Furthermore, they will not be complementary in any way and there will not be any substitution from one to the other. The expertise required of potential suppliers is similar for both markets in terms of technology, manufacturing, marketing and distribution. Therefore, your division and your competitors are the most likely suppliers of Vodites. Although the Sonite and Vodite technologies are similar, all firms will have to engage substantial R&D resources in order to develop their first Vodite product; recent calculations suggest that an investment of about 10 million dollars may be required for each Vodite.

| Firm | Brand | New or modified | Physical characteristics | | | | | Base cost ($) | Retail price ($) |
			Weight (Kg)	Design (Index)	Volume (Dm3)	Max Freq (KHz)	Power (W)		
A	SAMA	No	17	6	92	23	32	105	204
	SALT	No	17	7	75	35	65	176	279
	SAND	No	14	4	50	40	85	198	514
E	SEMI	Modified	14	5	50	40	80	197	565
	SELF	No	14	5	50	40	80	197	550
	SEBU	No	13	7	40	40	75	197	420
	SERT	No	13	7	50	30	55	198	478
I	SIBI	Modified	19	8	60	36	66	187	271
	SIPE	Cost impr.	20	7	70	15	30	91	203
	SICK	Modified	19	8	60	36	66	187	290

Figure 8 – A typical list of marketed brands

Experts tend to agree that the main physical characteristics of a Vodite will be the ones described in Figure 9. Finally, it is anticipated that the Vodite market could be quite attractive if the right products were made available at the right price.

Characteristics	Unit	Feasible range
Autonomy	Meter (m)	5 – 100
Maximum frequency	Kilohertz (kHz)	5 – 20
Diameter	Millimeter (mm)	10 – 100
Design	Index	3 – 10
Weight	Gram (g)	10 – 100
Base cost	$	10 +

Figure 9 – Vodite main physical characteristics

3.5 Naming Conventions

In Markstrat Online, brand names are made up of four characters, as shown in the figure below. The first letter must be an 'S' for a Sonite or a 'V' for a Vodite. The second letter identifies the firm marketing the brand and must be a vowel (A, E, I, O, U or Y). Finally, the last two characters can be letters or numbers, and can be freely chosen by each firm to generate different brand names.

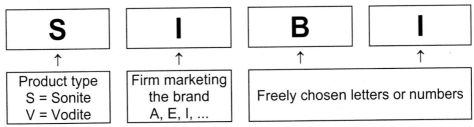

For instance, brands SIBI and SIRO would be Sonites marketed by firm I, and brand VAIN would be a Vodite marketed by company A. All new brands must follow these conventions, and must have different names. The selected name has no influence on the market response to the brand.

3.6 Sonite Customers

Sonite customers are adults who purchase the products for personal or professional use. Market research studies show that the Sonite market can be divided into five major groups of customers, or segments, having similar needs and purchasing behavior.

- ***Buffs (Bu)*** - People in this segment show a high level of interest in Sonites and other similar products. They are extremely knowledgeable about Sonite technology and the different characteristics of the existing brands. Buffs were probably among the first to use Sonite products. They demand high-performance products, but are less concerned by the convenience of the products. However, they are quite price-sensitive, since they use Sonite products for their personal use and do not necessarily have high incomes.

- **Singles (Si)** – As the name of this segment indicates, Singles live alone. They demand average levels of both performance and convenience in Sonite products. Like Buffs, they use Sonite products for personal purposes and are quite price-sensitive.

- **Professionals (Pr)** – Individuals in this segment may use Sonite products for both personal and professional reasons. As a consequence, they are looking for high quality, high-performance and easy-to-use products. They can afford expensive products and often view price as an indication of quality.

- **High earners (Hi)** – This group is characterized by their high incomes, using Sonite products on a private basis. Studies show that they usually buy fairly expensive products, which they can afford, and that their purchase is partially motivated by social status. Although they tend to use their Sonites less than the average consumer, they demand performance and convenience from the products.

- **Others (Ot)** – This segment includes all consumers who do not belong to any of the above groups. Although this segment is the largest and is composed of several sub-groups, most customers have similar needs. They are looking for cheap, low-performance products with average convenience. Experts believe that the penetration of this segment is not as high as the other segments. As a consequence, its future growth rate could exceed forecasts.

Each segment has specific needs in terms of physical characteristics and price. Awareness levels and purchase intentions vary significantly for existing products from one group to the other. Market forecast studies show that the sizes and growth rates of the five segments are significantly different. This is explained in part by the development stage of each segment, by the varying product offerings, and by the intensity of marketing effort targeted at each segment.

3.7 Vodite Customers

While potential consumers for Vodites are the same individuals as those who buy Sonites, a different segmentation scheme is likely to be valid for Vodites. Further studies need to be completed, but marketing experts believe that it will be more effective to group consumers according to how they adopt new products. In this light, three groups might be considered for Vodites.

- *Innovators (In)* – These consumers will be the first users of Vodite products. People in this segment tend to be adventurous and are willing to try new ideas at some risk. Although this segment will probably be the largest one in the early days, it represents only a small percentage of the total potential consumers. However, they demonstrate both a high desire and interest for Vodite products and their income levels are above average.

- *Early adopters (Ad)* – Consumers in this segment will not adopt Vodite products as quickly as innovators but will certainly do so before a majority of people have accepted the new technology. As this group is usually much larger than the previous one, its influence on other consumers is fairly high. Early adopters tend to be opinion leaders and helpful in 'advertising' the new product to other potential buyers. They are critical to the adoption process, and should not be neglected by marketers. They have an average income level.

- *Followers (Fo)* – These individuals represent the bulk of potential consumers. Because they perceive more risk in buying new products, they adopt a product innovation only after a large number of consumers have tried it. Innovators and early adopters particularly influence followers. Their income level is usually below average.

3.8 Distribution Channels

Sonite consumers tend to shop in the following three distribution channels and the same is likely to hold for Vodites:

- **Specialty stores** - These stores are usually small and do not belong to organized chains. They are geographically close to their customers and can provide a high level of service and technical support. As they do not distribute many different product categories, Sonite products account for a large proportion of their sales. These stores usually carry a broad product line for each category, including the most expensive and/or high-performance products. Because of their high level of technological expertise, specialty stores are likely to be the preferred distribution channel for Vodite products.

- **Department stores** - Department stores are characterized by the wide product assortment they offer. They usually have a department carrying Sonites. They provide extensive customer service, but their technological expertise is lower than that of specialty stores. Department stores are often organized in chains that have a degree of power in negotiating margins with manufacturers.

- **Mass Merchandisers** - These stores operate on a low-price, high-volume basis and try to minimize overheads. As a consequence, the level of service offered is lower than that of the two other channels. While mass merchandisers carry many different product categories, the depth of each product line is usually restricted to a few units. They often distribute the cheaper, low-performance products. Their lack of technical expertise and the low level of service may well prevent them from distributing Vodites in the early years.

As far as the Sonite market is concerned, market research studies show that all three distribution channels are important; therefore each of them should be visited by the companies' sales forces. There are approximately 30,000 specialty stores, 7,000 department stores belonging to 15 different chains, and 10,000 mass merchandisers belonging to 8 different chains.

Differences between margins obtained by the stores in each of the three channels are mainly due to differences in the level of service and volume sold. These margins are applied to retail prices and are approximately constant across brands for a given channel. In MARKSTRAT the distributor margins are: 40% for specialty stores; 30% for department stores; and 30% for mass merchandisers.

4. Managing Your Firm

The Marketing department for which you and your team will be working is responsible for the design and implementation of the marketing strategy of your division. You will have to decide the overall orientation of the company regarding:

- the *product portfolio strategy* – which brands the company is going to develop and market;

- the *segmentation and positioning strategy* – which market segments will be targeted and how products will be positioned;

- the *marketing mix strategy* – the day-to-day operational marketing decisions such as pricing, production, communication and distribution.

You will manage the Marketing department as a profit center, and your performance will be measured by the following indicators: net contribution generated, brand market shares, your ability to grow the firm revenues, quality of R&D projects successfully completed, etc. Finally, the best measure of your company's success will be its *stock price index*, a measure that takes all of the above indicators into account.

This chapter describes the decisions you will have to make each period. Before making dramatic changes, you should try to get a feel for the behavior of the market. Do not jump hastily to conclusions and bear in mind that obvious solutions may be based upon an incomplete analysis. To reach more robust decisions, use the information from market research studies to analyze your situation and past competitive behavior.

4.1 Production

Each period, you are responsible for submitting a production plan for each of your marketed brands. In the case of a relatively unsuccessful brand you may also decide to decrease the inventory, by selling all or part of it to a trading company.

The Production department is working for several divisions of your company, and can thus be viewed as a highly flexible external supplier. As a consequence, you are not concerned about manufacturing investments, fixed costs or capacity utilization. From one period to the next, you are completely free to increase or decrease the production planning of a given product, without any penalty. The Production department will always manufacture the required quantities in the best possible conditions.

In a given period, the actual production level for each product is automatically adjusted in response to actual demand for that product, within plus or minus 20% of the production plan submitted by Marketing. Figure 10 gives a few examples for varying situations of inventory, production plan and market demand (all numbers are in units).

	A	B	C	D
Beginning Inventory	8 000	8 000	25 000	0
Production Plan	100 000	120 000	100 000	80 000
Potential Sales	112 000	154 000	95 000	54 000
Actual Production	104 000	144 000	80 000	64 000
Actual Sales	112 000	152 000	95 000	54 000
Lost Sales	0	2 000	0	0
Ending Inventory	0	0	10 000	10 000

Figure 10 – Inventory and production plan versus market demand

The flexibility of the Production department goes beyond automatic adjustment of production plans. The units produced are charged to the Marketing department only when they are sold to distributors. The price paid to production is called the *transfer cost*, it incorporates all costs associated with this high level of flexibility, including depreciation and fixed costs. Units produced in excess are kept in inventory, and inventory-holding costs are charged to the Marketing department. Inventory costs per unit are calculated as a percentage of the transfer cost that can be found in the Newsletter.

The transfer cost of a given product increases with inflation. On the other hand, it decreases over time because of experience effects and economies of scale. As a rule of thumb, you can expect the transfer cost to be reduced by about 15% each time the cumulative production of a given product is doubled.

4.2 Pricing

In Markstrat Online, you must set the *recommended retail price* for each marketed brand. The retail price is the list price for consumers. The *average selling price* is the price at which you sell your product to distributors. It varies by distribution channel since different margins hold in each of the three channels, as explained in section 3.8.

Specialty and department stores tend to respect the recommended retail prices set by the firms. However, mass merchandisers use promotions or special offers to sell products that, on average, are equivalent to a discount rate of 10% off the list price. As a consequence, in absolute terms, mass merchandisers' margins are lower than those of the other two channels because the percentage margin applies to discounted prices. Figure 11 provides a summary of retail prices, margins and discounts.

		Recommended Retail Price = $ 400		
		Specialty Stores	Department stores	Mass Merchandisers
Actual retail price	$	400	400	360
Distribution margin	%	40%	30%	30%
	$	160	120	108
Selling price	$	240	280	252
Transfer cost	$	123	123	123
Unit gross contribution	$	117	157	129

Figure 11 – From retail price to unit contribution

Dumping is strictly forbidden in the Markstrat Online world; therefore the recommended retail price must be set so that the lowest selling price of a product is higher than its transfer cost. Finally, price increases or decreases greater than 30% in one period are highly discouraged as they often result in negative market reactions. On one hand, an excessive price increase is usually not accepted by consumers who may react strongly and stop purchasing the brand. On the other hand, an excessive price decrease will result in a proportional cut in the distributors' margin, and your salespeople may have a hard time finding distributors for the brand. A message will warn you when such decisions are made. *If you ignore the warning, the recommended retail price will be automatically adjusted up or down to stop such adverse reactions.*

4.3 Communication

You must make several communication decisions each period. First, you should determine the advertising budget allocated to each brand. This budget will be used to purchase media space and time. Second, you must specify the budget allocated to advertising research. This finances the creative work, media selection, or other activities conducted by advertising agencies which improve the quality of your message. In past years, companies have devoted on average 7% of their total communication expenditures to advertising research. Advertising research will usually make your advertising more effective, and is especially important when you introduce a new brand or when you want to reposition an existing one. In these last two instances, higher percentages are recommended (in the range of 15 to 20%).

Third, you are required to specify which segments should be targeted with your advertising. This way, the advertising agency will select the most appropriate media vehicle for the targeted segments.

Finally, you must define perceptual advertising objectives for each brand. This enables you to convey a *perceptual message* and emphasize, for instance, how weak a given brand is, or how powerful another one is. Section 7.3 is devoted to brand positioning through advertising and explains how to set perceptual objectives.

4.4 Sales Force

Your sales force is organized in three groups; each group is specialized to focus on the stores of a single distribution channel. The marketing department must specify the number of salespeople in each group. Salespeople may be reallocated from one distribution channel to another at no cost. Hiring or firing costs will be automatically charged to your department when the total number of salespeople increases or decreases.

Each of your sales representatives carries the entire line of products marketed by your firm. However, you must instruct them on how to allocate their time and efforts across the various brands in your portfolio.

4.5 Ordering Market Research Studies

One of your decisions will be to order market research studies. All studies are ordered at the beginning of a period and are conducted by a specialized research firm during that period. The results are delivered with your annual report at the end of the period.

• Consumer survey	• Competitive sales force estimates
• Consumer panel	• Industry benchmarking
• Distribution panel	• Advertising experiment
• Semantic scales	• Sales force experiment
• Multidimensional scaling	• Market forecast
• Competitive advertising estimates	• Conjoint analysis

Figure 12 – Available market research studies

All of the studies you purchase can be available on paper and/or on screen. The information provided is relevant to the market situation during the analyzed period, with the exception of the market-forecast study. The list of available studies is given in Figure 12 and all studies are detailed further in section **5.3**.

All studies except *Industry benchmarking* apply specifically to either the Sonite or Vodite market. Consequently, a maximum of 23 different studies may be ordered each period.

4.6 Research & Development

The Marketing department is responsible for initiating research & development projects. Making R&D decisions is a crucial task because: (1) existing products will probably have to be improved during their lifetime to suit the changing needs of consumers; (2) new products may have to be designed in order to target untapped segments in existing or new markets.

When launching a new R&D project, the Marketing department must specify the desired characteristics for the new or improved product, including the target transfer cost. You must also allocate a budget to each project. The R&D department is responsible for conducting the actual research & development work. Section 7.5 is devoted to the interface between the Marketing and Research & Development departments.

4.7 Marketing Budget

Each period, the marketing department is allocated a budget to cover its expenses as shown in the table below:

ADVERTISING	SALES FORCE	R & D	MARKET RESEARCH
• Advertising Media • Advertising Research	• Operating Cost • Hiring & Training Costs • Firing Costs	• Development Budgets	• Study Costs

Your marketing budget is linked to the success of the department, being equal to 40% of the net contribution generated in the previous period. However, there is a maximum level above which resources are reallocated to other divisions of the company to maximize the return on investment at the corporate level. Similarly, there is a minimum budget level for each period, whereby headquarters may effectively subsidize your division if you are not generating sufficient contribution internally so your division can continue operations.

In general, your budget for each period will be between $7,000,000 and $20,000,000. You will have to work within this given budget! If total spending exceeds the allocated budget for a period, expenses will be automatically cut, starting with advertising expenditures.

Note that if your objective is to maximize your return on investment, you should not necessarily spend your entire budget in every situation. If you perform outstandingly, you may be granted a large budget; however, spending it completely might be a waste of money.

5. Understanding Your Annual Report

You will receive your annual report at the beginning of each decision round. This report provides you with the results of the period that just ended. For instance, you will be making decisions for period 5 based on the annual report of period 4. The annual report is composed of three separate documents: the *Industry Newsletter*, the *Company Report* and the *Market Research Studies*. While reading this chapter, we suggest that you refer to the sample annual report in chapter 9 of this manual.

5.1 Industry Newsletter

The Industry Newsletter provides general and financial data on the industry, on the competing firms and on marketed brands. This is publicly held information; i.e. all competing firms have access to the same Industry Newsletter. The Newsletter consists of three or four sections, depending on the availability of Vodite brands.

Stock market and key performance indicators (page 89) – This section provides comparative charts with various financial and marketing performance indicators such as: market shares, sales, contributions, stock price indices and return on investment ratios. All numbers are given in absolute values and shows the percentage change from the previous period.

Economic variables and costs (page 90) – The evolution of economic variables such as the inflation rate and GNP growth rate are highlighted in this part of the Newsletter. Various costs relative to the market research studies, salespeople, and inventory are also provided.

Information on Sonite market (page 91) – This section details the physical characteristics and price of all marketed Sonite products, and it indicates which brands have been recently improved upon or introduced. It also provides the market shares (in units and in dollar value), the volume sold and the retail sales of all Sonite products. Volume and retail sales are given in absolute values and shows the percentage change from the previous period.

Information on Vodite market (page 92) – The same data as above is provided for any Vodite products on the market.

5.2 Company Report

The Company Report provides confidential company information. You and your team members are the only ones who have access to the information disclosed in your company report, with the exception of data given in the *Industry Benchmarking* study. The company report is comprised of the following five sections.

- Company results

- Brand results

- Research & Development results

- Cumulative results

- Decision summary

Company results (page 94) – The *Company Scorecard* is included in this section. It provides various financial and marketing performance indicators such as: market shares, sales, contributions, stock price index and return on investment ratios. All numbers are given in absolute values, show the percentage change from the previous period and show the percentage change since period 0. This section also incorporates the *Company Performance* statement, illustrated in Figure 13. This chart is a simplified Profit and Loss statement for your company; the basic financial elements are explained next.

Brand results (page 96) – This section provides the *Contribution by Brand* chart, detailed in Figure 14. This chart is similar to the *Company performance* chart; it provides financial elements for each marketed brand, as explained in the table below. This section also shows the total market share of each brand, and its distribution coverage, i.e. the number of stores carrying the brand.

Research & Development results (page 98) – This section provides the list of all R&D projects launched in the previous periods and provides the following details for each project. Figure 15 shows a list of R&D projects and additional explanations on how to read this chart.

Cumulative results (page 99) – Cumulative results on sales, production and marketing are provided in this section. It includes cumulative data since period 0, for all of the brands introduced and marketed since that time. Company performance results are also provided in the same format as the one illustrated in Figure 13.

Decision summary (page 100) – This section recalls the decisions that your team made at the beginning of the current period: brand management, sales force management, R&D projects and the market research studies purchased. In period 0, the previous management team made these decisions.

	Unit	Total	Sonite market	Vodite market
Sales				
Units sold	U	788 546	433 639	354 908
Average retail price	$	529	387	703
Average selling price	$	350	253	468
Revenues	K$	275 610	109 629	165 982
Production				
Units produced	U	747 100	371 400	375 700
Cost of goods sold	K$	-119 740	-53 048	-66 692
Inventory holding cost	K$	-458	-152	-306
Inventory disposal loss	K$	0	0	0
Contribution before marketing	K$	155 412	56 429	98 983
Marketing				
Advertising expenditures	K$	-12 204	-6 697	-5 507
Advertising research expenditures	K$	-1 657	-1 074	-583
Sales force	K$	-6 395	-4 210	-2 185
Contribution after marketing	K$	135 156	44 448	90 708
Other expenses				
Market research studies	K$	-1 018	-528	-453
Research and development	K$	-3 075	-1 975	-1 100
Interest paid	K$	0		
Exceptional cost or profit	K$	0		
Net contribution	K$	131 063		
Next period budget	K$	24 850		

Units sold	Number of units purchased by consumers.
Average retail price	Average price paid by consumers.
Average selling price	Average retail price – distributors' margins.
Revenues	Number of units sold x Average selling price.
Units produced	Number of units manufactured by the Production department.
Cost of goods sold (COGS)	Number of units sold x Average unit transfer cost.
Inventory holding cost	Units in inventory x Unit transfer cost x Inventory holding cost in %.
Inventory disposal loss	Loss incurred when selling inventory to a trading company.
Contribution before marketing (CBM)	Revenues – COGS – inventory costs – inventory disposal loss.
Contribution after marketing (CAM)	CBM – (advertising + advertising research + sales force).
Interest paid	Interest paid on loans granted in previous periods.
Exceptional cost or profit (ECP)	Exceptional items such as brand withdrawal costs.
Net contribution	CAM – (market research studies + R&D + interest + ECP).
Next period budget	40% of net contribution; minimum = M$ 7; maximum = M$ 20.

Figure 13 – Company results – Company performance

Sonite Brands Base R&D project	Unit	Total	SOLD PSOL2	SONO PSON2	SODU PSOSI	SODE PSOBU
Sales						
Units sold	U	433 639	132 025	83 061	177 174	41 378
Average retail price	$	387	454	535	261	415
Average selling price	$	253	304	343	171	256
Revenues	K$	109 629	40 147	28 516	30 368	10 597
Production						
Units produced	U	371 400	132 000	96 000	102 000	41 400
Current unit transfer cost	$	-	129	146	84	219
Average unit transfer cost	$	122	129	146	84	220
Cost of goods sold	K$	-53 048	-16 991	-12 087	-14 885	-9 085
Units in inventory	U	13 012	0	12 939	0	73
Inventory holding cost	K$	-152	0	-151	0	-1
Inventory disposal loss	K$	0	0	0	0	0
Contribution before marketing	K$	56 429	23 156	16 278	15 484	1 511
Marketing						
Advertising expenditures	K$	-6 697	-2 001	-1 496	-2 005	-1 195
Advertising research expenditures	K$	-1 074	-299	-204	-326	-245
Sales force	K$	-4 210	-1 814	-1 032	-960	-404
Contribution after marketing	K$	44 448	19 042	13 546	12 192	-333

Units sold	Number of units purchased by consumers.
Average retail price	Average price paid by consumers.
Average selling price	Average retail price – distributors' margins.
Revenues	Number of units sold x Average selling price.
Unit transfer cost	Price paid by Marketing to Production for each unit sold.
Cost of goods sold (COGS)	Number of units sold x Average unit transfer cost.
Units in inventory	Number of units produced but not sold at end of a period.
Inventory holding cost	Units in inventory x Unit transfer cost x Inventory holding cost in %.
Inventory disposal loss	Loss incurred when selling inventory to a trading company.
Contribution before marketing (CBM)	Revenues – COGS – inventory holding costs – inventory disposal loss.
Contribution after marketing (CAM)	CBM – (advertising + advertising research + sales force).

Figure 14 – Brand results – Brand Contributions

	Physical Characteristics					Base Cost $		Allocated Budget K$	
Name	Weight (Kg)	Design (Index)	Volume (Dm3)	Max Freq (KHz)	Power (W)	Current	Minimum realistic	Cumulative	Req. for completion
PSOLD	13	7	45	30	75	203	166	1 500	Avail. in P-1
PSONO	16	4	75	48	88	224	176	2 000	Avail. in P-1
PSOPR	16	5	75	40	75	176	158	963	Avail. in P2
PSOSI	16	7	75	34	54	142	134	1 050	Avail. in P2
PSON2	14	5	50	40	77	192	166	810	Avail. in P4
PSODU	16	7	75	36	63	148	147	940	Avail. in P6
PSOL2	14	7	38	30	55	165	141	756	Avail. in P5
PSOBU	15	7	40	38	77	205	175	918	Avail. in P5
PSON3	14	6	50	40	80	174	174	100	990
PSOD2*	16	7	40	35	77	205	173	550	Avail. in P7
PSOU2*	16	7	78	43	54	148	140	925	Avail. in P7
PSOL3*	14	7	38	25	55	165	138	500	Avail. in P7

(*) Projects written in bold font have just been completed this period.

- **Column 1** – Project name.
- **Columns 2 to 6** – The physical characteristics of the future product. This data is given in the relevant units for each characteristic: kilograms for weight, watts for power, etc.
- **Columns 7 and 8** – The *current* and the *minimum realistic base cost*. The base cost is the transfer cost at which the future product will be manufactured. It is calculated on the basis of an initial production batch of 100,000 units. The actual transfer cost will be higher than the base cost if the cumulated production is below 100,000 units, and lower than the base cost if the cumulated production is above 100,000 units. The minimum realistic base cost is the cost below which it is *impossible* to manufacture the future product (at least the first batch of 100,000 units). This minimum cost takes into account the purchase of raw materials, the labor required to manufacture the product and the depreciation of investments to be made in production processes.
- **Column 9** – The total cumulative budget invested so far in the project. Note that a project may be completed over several periods as explained in chapter 6.8.
- **Column 10** (project not completed) – The budget required to finish the project. This information is only relevant if the project is not completed. It indicates the additional budget that must be invested to ensure that the project will be completed in the following period. You may attempt to finish the project with a lower budget, but its successful completion is not guaranteed.
- **Column 10 (project completed)** – The period at which the project was completed.

Figure 15 – R&D – Project list

5.3 Market Research Studies

You may purchase up to 23 Market Research Studies each period. The following list provides a brief summary of information within each study.

Industry benchmarking (page 103) – The benchmarking report compiles general information from annual reports about each of the MARKSTRAT competitors. The same data is provided in a common format for all companies, in such a way that would allow you to compare competitive performance. The data provided includes sales, production costs, marketing expenditures and other expenses.

Consumer survey (page 104) – The consumer survey provides information on: (1) the level of *brand awareness* – the percentage of potential consumers in each segment who can spontaneously recall a given brand name; (2) *brand purchase intentions* – the percentage of potential consumers in each segment who intended to buy a given brand; (3) *shopping habits* – percentage of potential consumers in each segment who prefer to shop in a given distribution channel.

Consumer panel (page 105) – This study provides the total unit sales for each segment; the relative size of each segment; and the market shares, based on units sold, for each brand in each segment.

Distribution panel (page 106) – The distribution panel gives information on the total sales in units in each distribution channel; the relative size of each channel; and the market shares, based on units sold, for each brand in each channel. A second chart provides the distribution coverage for each brand in each channel, i.e. the percentage of stores carrying a given brand.

Semantic scales (page 107) – Semantic scales describe how consumers perceive the marketed brands. Respondents are asked to rate each brand along each physical characteristic on a scale from 1 to 7 according to the way they perceive the brand. For instance, a brand rated 2.3 on the Power scale is perceived as being less *powerful* than a brand rating 5.5 on the same scale. The study also provides the *ideal* ratings of each segment for each physical characteristic.

Finally, it provides the importance of each characteristic, in other words, the weight each characteristic holds in the buying decision. Additional charts and graphs are available in the simulation. For instance, you can obtain a graph representing the relationship between physical characteristics and perceptions, or a graph representing the evolution of customer needs since the beginning of the simulation.

Multidimensional scaling of brand similarities and preferences (page 108 to 110) – This is one of the most important studies that may be purchased. It provides a map showing the similarities and differences between marketed brands on three different dimensions. Two brands close to one another on the map are perceived as being similar. Inversely, two brands located in different quadrants are perceived as being significantly different; for instance, one may be perceived as less economical or as more convenient. Further information on perceptual maps and their interpretation will be explained in chapter 7.

Market forecast (page 111) – This study estimates the expected size in units and the growth rate of each segment for the next period as well as in five years time. These estimates are based on the current market situation and assume that no substantial changes such as brand introductions, or significant price increases or decreases will take place in the future. Consequently, depending on what actions are actually taken by your firm and your competitors, the resulting market size will either be higher or lower. For the new Vodite market, the estimates are based on interviews of potential consumers; these are less accurate and often turn out to be optimistic.

Competitive advertising estimates (page 112) – This study estimates the total advertising expenditures for each competitive brand by segment. (This study also provides the average advertising spending by brand and by firm, in total and for each segment).

Competitive sales force estimates (page 113) – This study estimates the number of salespeople allocated to each competitive brand, by distribution channel and in total. (It also provides the average sales force size by brand and by firm, in total and for each channel).

Advertising experiment (page 114) – This study estimates the effects of increasing your advertising budget by a given percentage. It projects brand awareness and market share for each of your brands. If for example, the advertising budget has been increased by 20% – assuming no change in other competitive actions, the resulting change in *contribution after marketing* is also provided. An increase in contribution for a given brand shows that you would have benefited from a higher level of advertising spending for this brand.

Sales force experiment (page 114) – The sales force experiment predicts the increased distribution coverage and market share for each of your brands, if the number of salespeople had been increased. For example, you may test the impact of adding 10 more salespeople – assuming no change in other competitive actions. The resulting change in *contribution after marketing* is also provided. An increase in contribution for a given brand shows that you would have benefited from allocating more salespeople to this brand.

Conjoint analysis (page 115) – This study is rather complex and expensive and is therefore not always made available to students. It provides the *utilities* – a real number between from 0 to 1 – of various levels for each of the four most important physical characteristics and for each segment. High utilities, for instance close to 1, demonstrate high consumer preferences for the corresponding physical levels.

6. Making Decisions

6.1 The Simulation Process

At the beginning of each decision round, you will be given your firm's annual *Company Report*, the *Industry Newsletter* and the *Market Research Studies* that you ordered in the previous period. The team should start by analyzing this information and agree on a strategy for the company. Once you have determined your marketing objectives, you will make decisions for the next period.

At the end of the decision round, you will submit your decisions to your instructor, together with the decisions of your competitors. The Markstrat Online software model will compile the data and generate the results of that period. These results will be reflected in your next Company Report, a new Industry Newsletter and new Market Research Studies.

After examining this new set of information, the team will review the objectives and decide whether to maintain or adapt the strategy. Your team will then make decisions for the next period, following this cycle of decisions and results for up to twelve simulated years.

6.2 Group Dynamics

During the first set of decisions, it is essential that you develop a good working relationship within your group. In the beginning it is important that each team member be involved in the discussion of all issues and that everyone develops a grasp of the business situation. For these reasons, try to avoid the inclination that each member concentrates in his or her area of expertise.

Later in the simulation, everybody will have developed a common understanding of the strategic issues. At the same time, the management of the firm will become more complex in terms of the number of brands, the R&D interface, the market developments, and the intensity of competition. Period 3 or 4 is usually a good time for each individual to start concentrating on some specific area of responsibility. In this way, the group will learn to work efficiently, and each of its members will benefit equally from the Markstrat Online experience.

6.3 Markstrat Online Main Screen

The Markstrat Online main screen is shown in Figure 16. Markstrat Online is a standard Microsoft Windows application like Word or Excel, with a menu bar at the top, a tool bar just below, and a main area to display charts, graphs or decision screens.

The pop-up menus at the top give you access to the main Markstrat Online menus; they are labeled:

Decisions, Report, Newsletter, Market studies, Analysis charts, Analysis tools, Interface

Decisions. This menu gives you access to the five main screens that should be used to make decisions: Brand Portfolio; Production, Price & Advertising; Sales Force & Distribution; Market Research Studies; and Research & Development. Each screen can be activated by first clicking on Decisions and by then selecting the corresponding sub-menu. Additional summary charts are available to help you make your decisions: Budget, Decision summary, Errors & warnings and Past decisions. The Marketing plan tool will help you calculate your company net contribution based on your current decisions and on sales estimates. Finally, New loan, Loan schedule and Budget increase or decrease will let you interface with the Bank or with the Corporate finance department to get loans or budget increases.

Report, Newsletter, Market studies. These menus provide the same information as the printed your annual report, plus a few additional graphs.

Analysis charts, Analysis Tools. These menus provide a comprehensive set of graphs and tools to help you analyze the market and competitive offerings.

Interface. With this menu you may upload or download files to and from the Markstrat Online remote server, and backup or restore files locally. You should use this menu to retrieve the latest results from the instructor and to transfer your decisions to the instructor. This menu is fully documented in chapter 2.

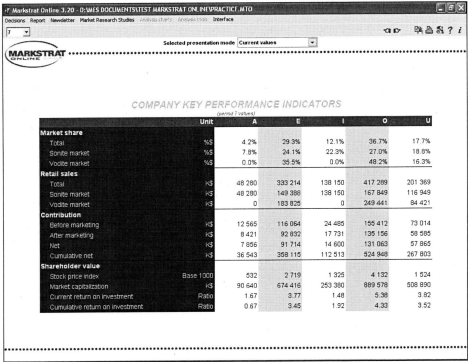

Figure 16 – Markstrat Online Main Screen

6.4 Brand Portfolio Decisions

The Brand portfolio decision screen is displayed in Figure 17. It enables you to introduce new brands and to modify or withdraw existing ones. The team may develop up to 5 Sonite brands and 5 Vodite brands per period.

Introducing a new brand

After clicking on the *Introduce new brand* button, a decision screen appears that will help you bring a new Sonite and Vodite brand to market. The name of the new brand must be entered using the naming conventions discussed in section 3.5. The name of a completed R&D project –giving the technical specifications for producing the brand– must be entered in the column *R&D project*, or it can be selected directly in the list of available R&D projects, which is provided for reference. Note that the specifications of each project can be obtained by clicking on the *View R&D report* button.

The *Undo* button can be used to remove a new brand added to the portfolio that you subsequently decide not to launch. Select the new brand and click on the *Undo* button to remove it from the *Marketed brands* list.

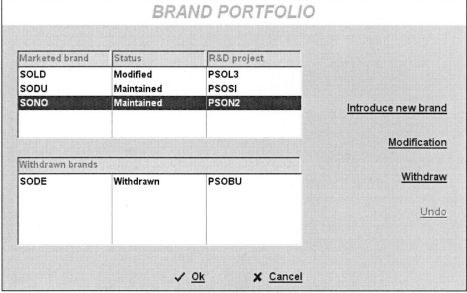

Figure 17 – Brand Portfolio decision screen

Modifying an existing brand

After selection of the brand to be modified, click on the *Modification* button. A decision screen appears. The R&D project name corresponding to the new product specification must be selected from the completed R&D projects. Naturally, the name of a modified brand does not change; otherwise, it would be a brand introduction.

The *Undo* button can be used to cancel the change made to a brand using the *Modification* button. Select the modified brand and click on the Undo button to retrieve the project on which the brand was based in the previous period.

Withdrawing a brand

The *Withdraw* option removes a brand that was marketed in the previous period. The brand will no longer be marketed or distributed to consumers. Select the brand to be removed in the *Marketed brands* list and click on the *Withdraw* button; the brand moves to the *Withdrawn brands* list.

If inventories remain when a brand is withdrawn from the market, they are sold to a trading company at a given percentage of the transfer cost and a loss is incurred. A brand that was marketed in the past and withdrawn from the market may not be reintroduced later in the simulation.

The *Undo* option enables you to cancel a brand withdrawal. Select the name of the withdrawn brand and then click on the *Undo* button.

6.5 *Production, Price & Advertising*

The Production, Price & Advertising decision screen is displayed in Figure 18. Clicking on the S or V drop-down (top left) switches between Sonite brands and Vodite brands. The brands that you have chosen to market next period are listed on the tabs at the bottom of the screen. Click on the tab of the brand to be displayed and enter your decisions for production, price, and advertising.

Production

Enter a production plan based on your sales forecasts for the upcoming period, taking into account any units left in inventory. The production department will adjust your plan by plus or minus 20% to respond to the actual market demand. If you are holding a high level of inventory, you can set the production plan to 0; but in this case, no automatic adjustment is possible.

Alternatively, you can decide to sell part of the inventory to a trading company which will buy it at a given percentage of its value, usually 50 to 80% hence, the loss incured for inventory disposal is usually between 20% and 50%. The exact percentage can be found in the Newsletter.

Price

Enter the *recommended retail price* in dollars, the list price of the brand. This corresponds to the price usually paid by consumers, except for shoppers using mass merchandisers which practice a 10% discount.

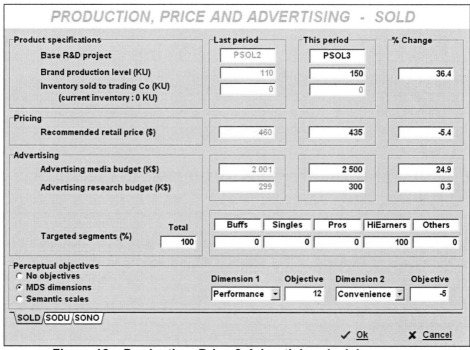

Figure 18 – Production, Price & Advertising decision screen

Advertising

Enter the *Advertising media budget*, to purchase media space, and the *Advertising research budget*, to improve the quality and the effectiveness of your advertising. Both budgets must be given in thousands of dollars. Then, allocate your advertising budget to the various market segments, by indicating the proportion of the budget targeted to each segment. The percentages must add to 100%.

Perceptual objectives

When looking to reposition a brand with advertising, as explained in section 7.3, you need to inform the advertising agency of the desired perceptual objectives for the brand. This is a complex decision that you will not have to make in the first period. You can skip this paragraph until you have reviewed the appropriate conceptual session with your Instructor, or until you have read and understood chapter 5.

If the advertising objective is simply to raise brand awareness without changing the perception of the brand, select the *No objectives* option.

Perceptual objectives may be chosen on any two communication dimensions. They may be provided either in terms of semantic scales or in terms of the composite dimensions given by the multidimensional scaling study. Just click on the scale of your choice: *MDS dimensions* or *Semantic scales*. Then, your chosen dimensions can be selected in boxes *Dimension 1* and *Dimension 2*. Finally, the levels objective for each desired position on each dimension must be entered. For the scales based on the multidimensional scaling study, these numbers should be between −20 and +20. For the semantic scales, the range is from 1 to 7, with one decimal point.

These perceptual objectives convey primarily qualitative information for the design of the advertising platform and copy (for example, to emphasize the light weight nature of the product). The numeric representation of these perceptual objectives is used only for communication purposes.

The communication may also be focused on a single dimension (a unique selling proposition). In this case, pick *None* in the list box of *Dimension 2* to indicate that the communication is on a single dimension indicated in the box of *Dimension 1*.

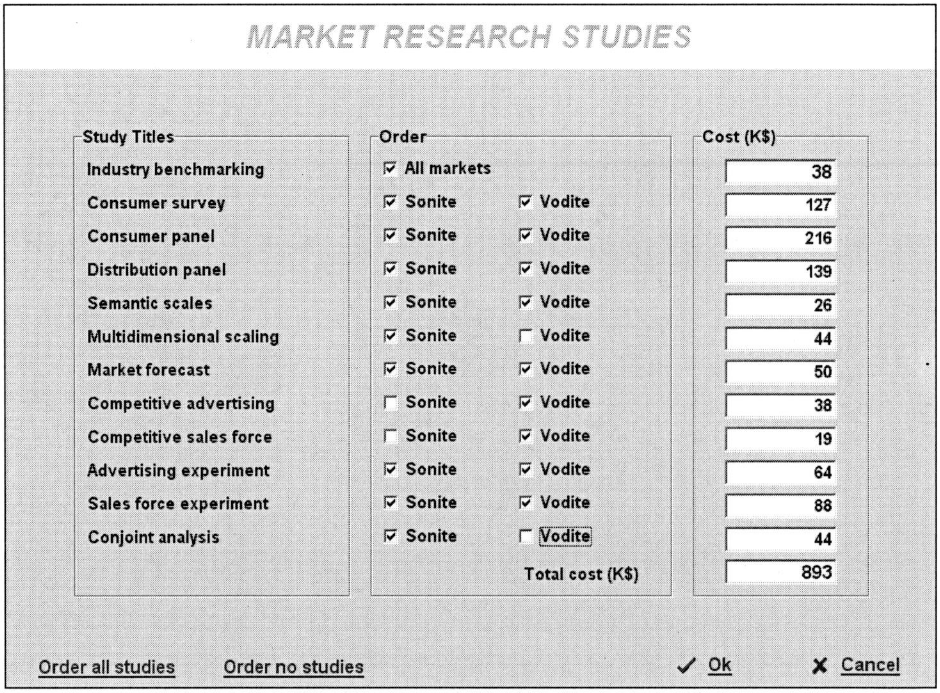

Study Titles	Order		Cost (K$)
Industry benchmarking	☑ All markets		38
Consumer survey	☑ Sonite	☑ Vodite	127
Consumer panel	☑ Sonite	☑ Vodite	216
Distribution panel	☑ Sonite	☑ Vodite	139
Semantic scales	☑ Sonite	☑ Vodite	26
Multidimensional scaling	☑ Sonite	☐ Vodite	44
Market forecast	☑ Sonite	☑ Vodite	50
Competitive advertising	☐ Sonite	☑ Vodite	38
Competitive sales force	☐ Sonite	☑ Vodite	19
Advertising experiment	☑ Sonite	☑ Vodite	64
Sales force experiment	☑ Sonite	☑ Vodite	88
Conjoint analysis	☑ Sonite	☐ Vodite	44
		Total cost (K$)	893

Order all studies   Order no studies   ✓ Ok   ✗ Cancel

Figure 19 – Market Research Study decision screen

6.6 *Market Research Studies*

The Market Research Studies decision screen is displayed in Figure 19. To purchase market studies, simply check the boxes that correspond to the studies you would like. The cost of these studies appear as the boxes are checked.

When you order a study, the research is performed during the next simulated period and the results are made available at the end of the period. This information is available for the following period's decisions.

Some of the studies may apply only if there are brands marketed during the period (e.g., the consumer panel for the Vodite market). You can use the Benchmarking study to anticipate whether competition will launch new brands. Moreover, if you order these studies and if no brands were marketed in the period, you will not be charged for them.

6.7 Sales Force and Distribution

The Sales Force and Distribution decision form is displayed in Figure 20. Your company's sales force is organized by distribution channel. You will have to make two decisions: (1) how many salespeople to assign to each distribution channel; and (2) how to allocate the sales force effort across brands.

Number of salespeople

Enter the number of salespeople assigned to each distribution channel. Changes in the number of salespersons are expected to have an influence on the distribution coverage of your brands. Since your sales force is knowledgeable about all your products, you can modify the allocation of salespeople across distribution channels at no cost.

Percentage of efforts

Instruct your salespeople in a given channel on how to allocate their efforts between your firm's brands. This decision is important since some brands are targeted to segments which are more likely to purchase goods in certain distribution channels. Entering percentages in the appropriate cells makes the allocation; the percentages must add up to 100%.

The *Assistant* button can help you allocate the sales force efforts automatically, according to four predefined rules. *Equal allocation across all brands* allocates an equal percentage of effort to each brand within a channel. The three other options, *Proportional to last period's unit sales*, *retail sales* or *contribution*, are based on the previous period's results. Note that using this feature, no sales effort will be allocated to new brands introduced during the current period. You will need to enter some figures so that a certain amount of effort is devoted to new brands.

Lastly, the *Normalize* button automatically adjusts your data to total 100% in each channel.

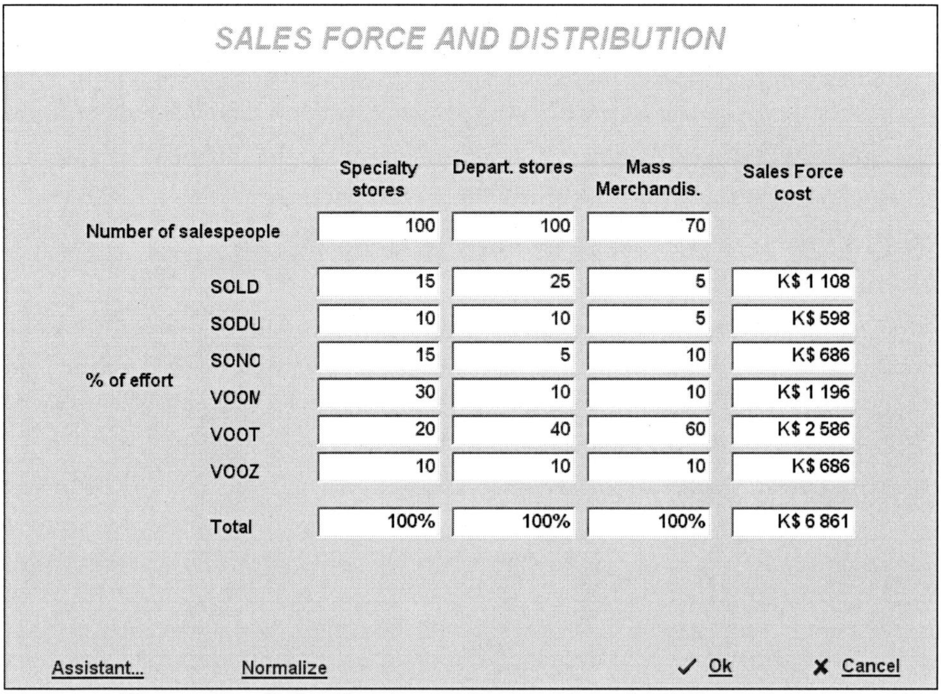
SALES FORCE AND DISTRIBUTION

		Specialty stores	Depart. stores	Mass Merchandis.	Sales Force cost
Number of salespeople		100	100	70	
% of effort	SOLD	15	25	5	K$ 1 108
	SODU	10	10	5	K$ 598
	SONO	15	5	10	K$ 686
	VOON	30	10	10	K$ 1 196
	VOOT	20	40	60	K$ 2 586
	VOOZ	10	10	10	K$ 686
	Total	100%	100%	100%	K$ 6 861

Assistant...
Normalize
Ok
Cancel

Figure 20 – Sales Force and Distribution decision screen

6.8 Research & Development

Research & Development decisions are quite complex. It is unlikely that these decisions will be necessary during your first period. You can skip this section until you have attended the appropriate conceptual session with your Instructor, or until you have read and understood chapter 5.

The Research & Development decision screen is displayed in Figure 21. Buttons at the bottom of the window are used to *start* new R&D projects; *shelve* an incomplete project; or *continue* a project that had been temporarily suspended. The projects that your R&D department will work on next period are listed on the tabs at the bottom of the screen. Clicking on the *S* or *V* drop-down at the top displays either Sonite or Vodite projects.

For each project, the values of the five physical characteristics for the desired future product must be entered in the corresponding cells. The range of technically feasible characteristics for each dimension is indicated in brackets. The *requested base cost* is the transfer cost that will be charged to the Marketing department for each unit of the future product, assuming a production batch of 100,000 units. You can ask the R&D department to seek the minimum transfer cost technically feasible by checking the box *Develop project at minimum base cost*. The allocated budget corresponds to the budget devoted to the project over the next period. The cumulative R&D budget is also indicated.

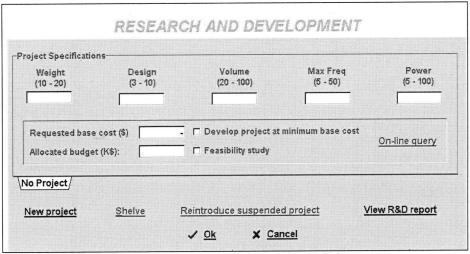

Figure 21 – Research & Development decision screen

You can order a *feasibility study* from the R&D department for $100,000. This study will tell you the minimum cost at which the product can realistically be manufactured, and the R&D budget required guaranteeing its completion at the currently requested base cost. A feasibility study takes one period, the information is provided in the next period within the R&D section of the company report.

Alternatively, you can initiate up to five *on-line queries per period*, which will give the same information as the feasibility studies, at no charge. However, these immediate results are often over-estimated by as much as 50%.

6.9 *Checking your Decisions*

Before submitting your decisions to the Instructor, it is suggested that you check that the program has not discovered any mistakes with your decisions. Three sets of charts will help you verify your decisions.

- **Budget (see Figure 22).** The budget charts provide details on how you have decided to spend your marketing budget in the upcoming period. At any time you can check your expenditures against your allocated budget. A warning message will appear if the budget is exceeded. This message should not be ignored; otherwise, the simulation will arbitrarily cut your expenditures, starting with advertising.

- **Summary (see Figure 23 and Figure 24).** The *Summary* button leads to five charts that provide a detailed description of all decisions made by your team.

- **Errors and Warnings (see Figure 25).** Errors indicate corrections that should be made because of inconsistent decisions, while warnings draw attention to possible problems. In these instances, you should check your decisions carefully to make sure that all entries are correct.

	Unit	Total	Sonite market	Vodite market
Advertising expenditures	K$	11 507	6 000	5 507
Advertising research expenditures	K$	1 408	825	583
Sales force				
Operating cost	K$	6 841	2 382	4 459
Hiring and training cost	K$	49	17	32
Firing cost	K$	0	0	0
Market research studies				
Market specific	K$	855	481	374
Other sudies	K$	38	-	-
Research and development	K$	4 720	2 240	2 480
Total expenditures	K$	25 418	11 945	13 435
Authorized budget	K$	24 850		
Capital borrowed from bank	K$	0		
Budget increase (+) or decrease (-)	K$	0		
Deviation from budget	K$		BUDGET EXCEEDED	

Figure 22 – Decisions – Overall marketing budget

DECISION SUMMARY - BRAND MANAGEMENT

Sonite Brands		SOLD	SODU	SONO	
Base R&D project		PSOL3	PSOSI	PSON2	
Production planning	KU	150	85	120	
Inventory sold to trading company	KU	0	0	0	
Recommended retail price	$	435	270	545	
Advertising budget	K$	2 500	2 000	1 500	
Advertising research budget	K$	300	325	200	
	Buffs	0	0	0	
	Singles	0	100	0	
Targeted segments in %	Professionals	0	0	100	
	High earners	100	0	0	
	Others	0	0	0	
Perceptual Objectives					
Dimension 1		Performance	Power	None	
Objective 1	[1,7] or [-20,+20]	12.0	4.0	-	
Dimension 2		Convenience	None	None	
Objective 2	[1,7] or [-20,+20]	-5.0	-	-	

Brand management / Sales force / Research and development projects / Market studies / Loan and Budget /

Figure 23 – Decisions – Brand management summary

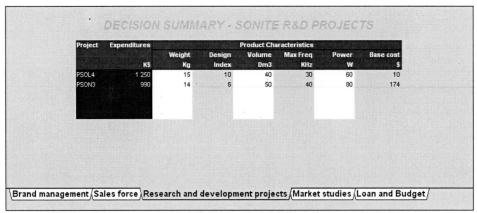

Figure 24 – Decisions – Research and development summary

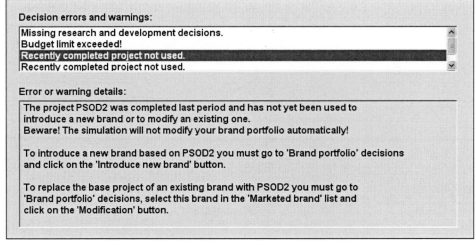

Figure 25 – Decisions – Errors & Warnings

6.10 Validating your decisions with the Marketing Plan Tool

After accessing the marketing plan section there are five distinct components which appear in the tabs at the bottom of the screen: Segment sizes, Brand shares/sales, Distribution mix, Brand contribution, and Company performance. Click on the corresponding tab accesses each component of the marketing plan. The first three correspond to the different types of estimates that you have to input into the plan. The last two provide estimated results based on both your decisions and your estimates.

Marketing Plan - Segment Sizes

The first estimates you must provide as inputs to the marketing plan concern the size (in thousands of units) of each segment. Click on the Segment sizes tab in the Marketing Plan section. The chart at the center of the screen initially displays each segment's size last period. The estimates for the variation of the segments' sizes next period should be entered in one of the two columns on the right-hand side, in thousands of units or in percentage change. One can shift from the Sonites screen to the Vodites screen with the selector drop down in the top left-hand corner of the dialog box.

Two automated estimation approaches are available. You can click on the "Same as last period" button to use segment's size from the previous period, or click on the "As in market forecast study" selection to input the segment size projections from market research. The second alternative is available only if the corresponding study has been purchased. If this is not the case, the selection is grayed. These two automated approaches provide a basis on which individual adjustments can be made, either in thousands of units or in percentage change.

Marketing Plan - Brand sales or brand share estimates by segment

One of the most important aspects of marketing planning is the anticipation of the market response to a specific set of decisions or actions. In this screen, anticipated market reactions must be entered for each brand in each segment. They can be specified either in terms of brand shares or brand sales by selecting the appropriate tab selection at the bottom of the screen. The numbers for the previous period are displayed for each brand in each segment as well as for the total market. An estimate for the next period can be entered either as a target or as a change from the previous period.

When making these estimates, make sure to take into account your own portfolio decisions as well as the ones of your competitors. In particular, brand introduction or upgrade should be examined closely so as to best estimate their impact on brand market shares.

Assuming that brand share inputs are first selected, one easy way to start is to use the same brand shares as in the previous period. Estimates can then be changed for each brand/segment combination, either as expected brand shares or as expected changes in brand share points. Whenever a change is made in any of the estimates, the number for the other mode of entry is automatically updated. The total brand share estimates for the market as a whole are also updated in the right-hand column. Simultaneously, the estimates of the corresponding brand unit sales in each segment are calculated based on the segment sizes previously defined and the brand share inputs. These numbers can be displayed by selecting the brand sales tab selection at the bottom of the screen. The estimates of brand sales can then be updated as targets or as changes from the previous period in the same way as for the brand shares.

The approach described above consists of:

    1. Starting with brand share estimates,

2. Displaying the expected brand sales resulting from the segment size and market share estimates, and

3. Updating selected brand sales estimates. It probably reflects the most logical process but it is also possible to directly set estimates of expected brand sales. In this case, brand share estimates are calculated on the basis of the brand sales and the segment sizes.

Marketing Plan - Distribution Mix

The price received by the firm for the sale of a product is equal to the retail price minus the distributor's margin. As the distribution margin varies across channels, the average selling price of a brand will depend on the mix of its sales across the channels. To calculate the financial contribution of a brand thus requires an estimate of its distribution mix.

Selecting the corresponding tab in the marketing plan section can make the Distribution mix estimates. They can be set to the same values as in the last period, or be calculated automatically based on the shopping habits study, by selecting the appropriate tab selection at the bottom center of the screen. The second alternative is available only if this market research study has been purchased in the current period. In this case, Markstrat Online uses the brand sales projections entered in the previous steps of the marketing plan. For each brand, the purchases of each segment are split by channel based on the shopping habits data. The sales of a brand in a given channel are obtained by total over the segments.

The distribution mix estimates can also be entered or updated manually one by one. One should, however, be particularly careful that the vertical sum of the percentages adds up to 100. The average distribution margin corresponding to a given mix is displayed on the bottom line and is updated any time a change is made in the chart.

Marketing Plan - Projections

On the basis of the decisions and the estimates for segment sizes, brand shares, brand sales, and the distribution mix, the marketing plan section can make financial projections for the next period. These projections can be displayed by selecting the Brand contribution and Company performance tabs at the bottom of the screen. When making financial projections, the software also makes a number of consistency checks; an errors and warnings screen may be displayed if any problems are encountered. Common inconsistencies include forgetting to enter some estimates, the distribution mix for a brand not adding up to 100%, or the sales forecast for a brand exceeding the available inventory volume plus the production plan. Such errors and warnings will require corrections in either the marketing plan estimates or the decisions. In the first case, just select the appropriate tab and make the desired adjustments before returning to the financial projections. In the second case, you can go back to the decision menu by clicking on the close selection at the bottom of the screen, make any needed changes to the decisions, and return to the marketing plan section. The previous estimates entered in this marketing plan section have been saved and will be used for financial projections unless modified.

Selecting the Brand contribution tab gives access, if all consistency checks are passed, to a pro forma statement of brand contribution. From the top line of the statement, units sold, to the bottom line, contribution after marketing, the software uses your decisions and estimates to produce a simulation of the brand contribution statement, which will appear in the company report. For instance, the average selling price is obtained from the retail pricing decision and the average distribution margin calculated from the distribution mix estimates. Similarly, the inventory level is calculated on the basis of the previous inventory (factual data) plus the production plan (a decision) minus the sales estimates, allowing for upward or downward adjustments possible in the production process. A separate brand contribution report is available for Sonites and Vodites, simply by selecting the Sonite or Vodite drop-down at the top of the screen.

Selecting the Company performance tab gives access, if all consistency checks are passed, to a pro forma statement of company performance. This replicates a page in the company report but allows you to go one step further by simulating results based on estimates. From the top line of units sold to the level of contribution after marketing, it is an aggregate of the information available in the brand contribution pro forma statement, separately for Sonites and Vodites as well as in total. Other expenses are then deducted to provide the net contribution. Finally, a budget for next period is estimated on the basis of these expected financial results.

Marketing Plan - The Planning Process

The MARKSTRAT marketing plan section is a useful tool to check the consistency of decisions and to easily anticipate their possible financial consequences. It provides, however, no guarantee of achieving the projected results. The actual brand contribution and company performance statements for the next period may be quite different from the pro forma projections obtained from the plan!

Many facets of the environment may have changed unexpectedly, including consumer needs or competitive actions. Other aspects directly controlled by the firm may not have been properly incorporated, or may have been overlooked. For example, students often overlook the following issues:

- the distribution mix estimates may not have taken into account the fact that the deployment of the firm's sales force no longer corresponds to the new shopping trends;

- or the share estimates for a given brand did not anticipate negative consumer reactions to the price increase;

- or the cut in the advertising budget did not have such a negative impact on sales and that, as a result, the brand has performed better than expected and is out of stock.

The process of planning in Markstrat Online brings discipline to marketing thinking, action, and learning in at least three important ways: firstly, by demanding a focus on the tangible results of decisions at the brand level; secondly by making it easy to check the validity of the overall financial results; and thirdly by providing support for a post-mortem analysis.

On the first aspect, the marketing plan section helps to focus on the three key elements of market evolution (segment sizes), brand performance (in shares or volume), and distribution coverage. Having to submit estimates for these components of the plan should solicit discussion and reflection about the variables affecting them. By modifying the estimates, it is also relatively convenient to perform sensitivity analyses to better understand how they affect the brand contribution. Moreover, if the resulting projected brand contribution appears significantly higher or lower than expected, then the validity of some of the decisions or estimates should be questioned. For instance, observing an abnormally high projected contribution for a given brand may lead to checking if the share estimate is coherent with the competitive positioning, the retail price, or the advertising support of the brand. It is easy to switch between the marketing plan section and the other components of the decision screen to adjust either the decisions or the estimates, and reach a situation in which the firm's management has confidence.

The marketing plan section of the Markstrat Online software also allows you to easily check on the expected overall financial performance of the firm. Within the firm's portfolio, it may be decided to invest heavily in a new brand and to accept a substantially negative contribution for this brand as long as other products generate sufficient funds to reach financial objectives. This financial interdependence between brands is sometimes difficult to apprehend but it is easy to investigate and analyze with the marketing plan section.

Finally, an important role of the marketing plan is to provide a tangible basis to learn over time. The Brand Contribution and Company Performance statements in the marketing plan are in the same format as in the company report. This makes it easy to compare between the anticipated projections and the actual results when they are obtained. A systematic analysis of the sources of variance between the two documents will help you learn both about the market mechanisms and about the planning process. In the long-term, this learning dimension is probably the most important contribution of the marketing planning process.

7. Positioning and Research & Development

As you may expect, the market environment will change during the course of the simulation. For instance, the needs of customers will probably evolve over time. (I.e. some segments may want more powerful brands while others may expect prices to fall). To respond to these changes, companies will have to introduce new Sonite or Vodite brands, and reposition or withdraw existing ones. As marketing resources are limited, it is extremely important to adopt optimal segmentation and positioning strategies, especially because a MARKSTRAT company cannot market more than five brands in a given period in each market. Your department will be faced with the following strategic issues on market segmentation and product positioning:

- Which segments to target?
- How to design products satisfying the needs of these segments?
- How to position new brands effectively?
- How to reposition existing brands to better fit customers' needs?

The goal of this chapter is to describe the various approaches that can be used in MARKSTRAT to address these issues.

7.1 Semantic Scales & Multidimensional Scaling

Technical experts can easily classify the marketed brands based on objective data such as technical attributes and prices. However, consumers who are about to make a purchase decision are influenced by their perceptions of the brands available on the market rather than by the actual features and properties of these brands.

Perceptions are by definition subjective and can therefore be distorted from reality. The Markstrat Online simulation provides two market research studies to assess consumers' needs and to estimate how brands are perceived: the *Semantic scales* study and the *Multidimensional scaling* study.

Semantic scales – This study describes how consumers perceive the marketed brands. Respondents are asked to rate the physical characteristics of each brand on a scale from 1 to 7. For instance, consumers have rated the brand SAND at 2.41 on the Power scale shown below because they perceive it as being less *powerful* than brand SILK, rated at 5.32 on the same scale.

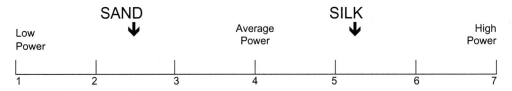

The study also provides the *ideal* rating for each characteristic and each segment. The results of this study are shown in Figure 26. By comparing the perceived ratings of your brand with the ideal ones for a given segment, you can determine if this brand fits the needs of customers in that segment. If not, you can compare its physical characteristics with those of the most preferred brands, and see how large the technical gap is. In order to bridge a significant technical gap, you will need to launch a new R&D project.

Note that even the most preferred brand may not be ideally positioned. In this case, you need to extrapolate what may be the ideal physical attributes (power, weight... price) for the targeted customer group. The graph shown in Figure 27 is provided in the simulation for each physical attribute when you purchase the Semantic scales study. *Perceptions are plotted against actual attributes for all marketed brands. A graphical interpolation on this graph will let you accurately calculate which physical level is required to reach a given perceived level.*

Segment	Weight	Design	Volume	Max Freq	Power	Price
Buffs	3.94	4.88	3.14	5.64	5.56	4.87
Singles	5.64	5.20	5.02	5.11	4.87	2.70
Pros	3.43	2.77	3.29	5.94	5.85	6.34
HiEarners	4.82	5.48	4.88	3.79	4.27	5.55
Others	5.24	4.05	6.02	3.47	2.71	2.05
Importance of characteristic (1)	1	4	2	3	6	10

(1) On a scale from 1 to 10 - 1 = Not important - 10 = Very important

Firm	Brand	Weight	Design	Volume	Max Freq	Power	Price
A	SAMA	5.47	3.03	6.05	3.00	2.61	2.12
	SALT	5.41	4.19	4.79	4.64	4.38	3.03
	SAND	3.52	1.86	3.41	5.64	5.99	5.99
E	SEMI	3.17	2.82	2.99	5.81	5.89	6.24
	SELF	3.59	2.04	2.82	5.99	5.96	6.27
	SEBU	2.71	4.60	2.44	5.78	5.55	4.83
	SERT	2.70	4.70	3.16	4.37	4.08	5.79
I	SIBI	6.45	5.66	4.00	5.04	4.69	2.65
	SIPE	6.50	4.27	4.86	2.24	2.71	2.06
	SICK	6.45	5.66	4.00	4.74	4.27	2.78
O	SOLD	3.26	4.60	2.35	4.36	4.19	5.58
	SONO	3.31	2.71	3.14	5.84	5.83	6.16
	SODU	4.68	4.92	5.20	5.16	4.68	2.61
	SODE	3.90	4.42	2.50	5.58	5.73	4.98
U	SUSI	5.37	3.22	6.18	3.34	2.52	2.09
	SULI	3.36	2.45	3.16	5.79	5.79	6.19
	SUBF	5.31	1.63	4.46	5.12	5.22	3.09

Figure 26 – Semantic scales study: Ideal values and brand perceptions

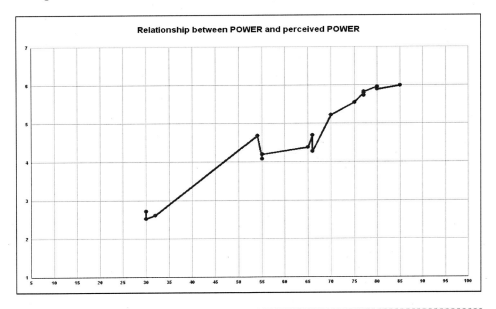

Figure 27 – Relationship between attributes and semantic scales

***Multidimensional scaling of brands similarities and preferences* –** This study provides a three-dimensional map showing the similarities and differences between marketed brands. This map is built through a complex process. First, respondents are asked to rate pairs of marketed brands according to the similarities or differences between two brands. Second, complex mathematical formulas are applied to these ratings to build a three-dimensional map where the distance between two brands is small for similar brands -brands that are close to each other on the map- and large for dissimilar brands -brands that are far from each other on the map. The map is a graphical representation of the respondents' ratings. Third, experts provide an interpretation for each of the three axes. Each axis is usually attached to a composite dimension like Convenience or Performance, i.e. a combination of several physical characteristics. Finally, respondents are asked to indicate what would be their ideal position on the map.

The result of this long process is shown in Figure 28. Note that only two dimensions out of the three can be represented simultaneously. The circles *Bu*, *Si*, *Pr*, *Hi*, and *Ot* on the graph represent the ideal points of the five segments. Each circle only represents the *center of gravity* of the whole segment. The various geometric shapes (square, triangle, star...) correspond to the positioning of the brands as they are perceived by the market at the time of the study. Each brand name is clearly labeled. One specific color and shape is attributed to each firm (for example, all brands marketed by firm A is represented by red stars).

For the Sonite market, the best interpretation of the three axes is given in the table below.

Axis	Composite Dimension	Relative importance	Influence of physical characteristics					
			Weight	Design	Volume	Max Freq.	Power	Price
1	Economy	High	Slight	Slight	Slight	Slight	Slight	**Strong**
2	Performance	Medium	Slight	Slight	Slight	Moderate	**Strong**	Slight
3	Convenience	Low	Moderate	**Strong**	Moderate	Slight	Slight	Slight

Note that for Weight, Volume, Diameter and Price, the relationship between the corresponding composite dimension and the attribute is an *inverse* function. For instance the lower the weight, the higher the perceived convenience or flexibility.

Experts have attempted to build the same table for the Vodite market and have come up with the following results, which should be used with care since no brands are marketed yet.

Axis	Composite Dimension	Relative importance	Influence of physical characteristics					
			Autonomy	Max Freq.	Diameter	Design	Weight	Price
1	Efficacy	High	Slight	Strong	Slight	Moderate	Slight	Slight
2	Flexibility	Medium	**Strong**	Slight	Moderate	Slight	Moderate	Slight
3	Economy	Low	Slight	Slight	Slight	Slight	Slight	**Strong**

Finally, this complex task cannot be achieved unless a significant number of brands are marketed. The MDS study is therefore not available for the Vodite market until a sufficient number of brands are marketed.

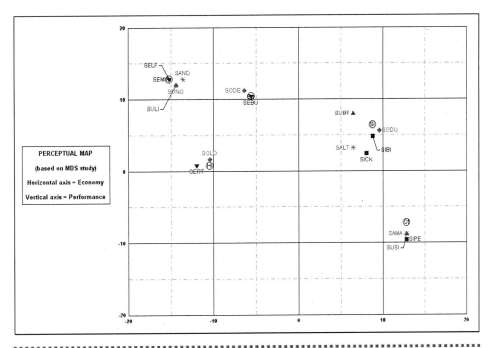

Figure 28 – Perceptual map

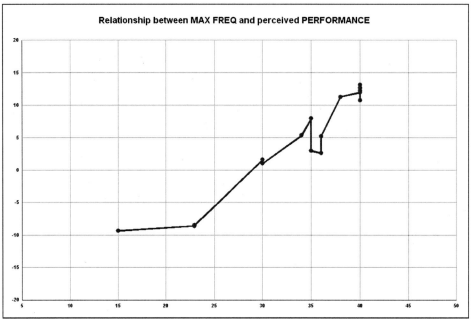

Figure 29 – Relationship between attributes and MDS perceptions

7.2 *Repositioning Strategies*

Ideal points on the perceptual map, or on the semantic scales' chart, reflect the needs of consumers, or the price that they are ready to pay to get a product that fits these needs. *For a given brand and a given segment, the optimal position on the map is as close as possible to the ideal point of that segment.* However, there are several reasons why brands are not always ideally positioned.

Changing segment needs

Segment needs evolve over time. This may be due to changes in the environment or in the consumers' value and behavior. Consequently, a brand which was well positioned when it was introduced on the market may now be perceived as *low-performance* or as *having an unnecessarily high frequency* a few periods later.

Period after period, the distance on the map between the brand and the ideal point becomes greater and greater.

Price pressure

This situation is similar to the previous one. As price is the most important dimension in the Sonite market, manufacturers should expect pressure from consumers to lower prices, especially in the low-end segments. Again, if brand prices are not adjusted accordingly, the distance between the brand and the ideal point along the price or economy axis is likely to increase.

New target segments

For a new market in its early stages, a good strategy may be to serve several segments with a single brand. This situation may occur if the needs of two segments are fairly similar or if one segment is too small to allow the necessary economies of scale. Then, as these needs change, or as the segment size increases, it may become necessary to position one brand closer to each ideal point.

Competitor entry

In the absence of competition, one firm may successful serve consumers with a product that is not exactly adapted to their needs. Then, if a competitor introduces a new brand that fits these needs better, it may become necessary to reposition the old brand closer to the ideal point.

In all the above situations, brands must be repositioned to adapt to new environmental conditions. Note that a brand does not always need to be repositioned on all dimensions. For instance, a two or three year old brand may now be perceived as low-performance, but as having the right convenience level. In this case, there is no reason to change the perception along the convenience dimension. Repositioning can be achieved by changing the brand's price, through advertising or via R&D.

7.3 Positioning with Advertising

Advertising in Markstrat Online is mainly used to build brand awareness and to inform customers about its physical characteristics. Advertising can also be used to reposition a brand. Although consumers' perceptions are linked to the brand's physical characteristics, they can be slightly influenced by communication. But the repositioning effect is limited; this is especially true when the brand awareness level is high, because a brand which consumers are extremely familiar with is more difficult to reposition. Beyond a certain level, brand repositioning can no longer be done by advertising alone, and it therefore becomes necessary to complete an R&D project with physical characteristics matching consumers' needs, and then to upgrade the brand. R&D projects will take at least one period to complete, while repositioning through advertising has an immediate effect.

Using advertising to reposition a product is a four step process:

1. Identify the target position on the perceptual map or on the semantic scales' chart.

2. Specify perceptual objectives for the brand when making *Production, Price & Advertising* decisions, as explained in section 6.5. You can choose to set perceptual objectives either on semantic scales or on MDS dimensions. For example, to reposition a brand closer to the *Singles* segment along dimensions Weight and Power, you must first try to estimate the future ideal positions of that segment on these two dimensions, by looking at the chart *Ideal value evolution* in the semantic scales study; then you must select the two chosen dimensions and enter the coordinates of the point that you want to reach on the semantic scales' chart. A maximum of two dimensions may be specified to keep the message simple and effective.

3. Allocate an advertising media budget for the brand, to buy media space and time, and an advertising research budget. The effect of advertising research is two-fold. First, it makes your advertising campaign more effective, by a better selection of media and a better design of the advertising copy. Second, the repositioning impact will be higher in terms

of reaching the perceptual objectives, although there will naturally be a limit as to how far and how fast advertising can change perceptions.

4. Indicate the percentages allocated to the *Targeted segments*. Obviously, the targeted segments must be coherent with the perceptual objectives. However, this decision alone is not sufficient to reposition a brand. Targeting specific segments is mainly done by selecting the most appropriate media to communicate the message, but it has little effect on the *content* of the message.

Finally, you will have to implement the same type of advertising program when you change the physical characteristics of a brand – by implementing a new R&D project – or when you increase or decrease its price significantly, to inform the consumers about these new characteristics and price.

7.4 Positioning through Research & Development

As explained before, a brand must be repositioned through R&D when the distance on the perceptual map – or on the semantic scales' chart – between the brand and the target segment's ideal position is too large. Research and development must also be used to introduce new brands, since all marketed brands must be based on R&D projects.

Using R&D to reposition a product or to introduce a new one is a four step process:

1. Identify the target position on the perceptual map or on the semantic scales' chart.

2. Estimate the physical characteristics that correspond to this target position. This can be done in at least three different ways.

   – The best solution is to use one of the two charts plotting the relationships between physical attributes (power, weight... price) and semantic scales or coordinates on the perceptual map. These two charts are provided in the simulation, one with the semantic scales study (see Figure 27), and the other one with the MDS study (see Figure 29). A simple graphical interpolation on the appropriate chart will let you calculate quite accurately which physical level is required to reach a given semantic scale or a given MDS position.

-   These charts may not be available when only a few brands are marketed. This is likely to be true in the early stages of the Vodite market. In this case, the best solution is to simply estimate the optimal physical characteristic for a given segment from the closest brand available in the market. For instance, on the map in Figure 28, brand SODU appears to have the appropriate Performance level for the Singles segment, and brand SAMA for Others segment.

-   The perceptual map is not available when no brands are marketed. However, you may still obtain information on segment needs from the semantic scales study. Consumers may for instance indicate that they are looking for brands with a high autonomy, rated 5.5 on the 1 to 7 scale. Your best option is to assume that there exists a linear relationship between autonomy in meters and semantic scales, i.e. that the lowest autonomy (5 meters) would be rated 1, and that the highest autonomy (100 meters) would be rated 7. In this case, the conversion formulas are:

$$S = [(X-LB) / (UB-LB)] \times 6+1 \quad \textbf{OR} \quad X = \{[(S-1)/6] \times (UB-LB)\} + LB$$

where S is the target semantic scale, X is the corresponding physical level, and LB and UB are the lower and upper limits of the physical characteristic's feasible range. In the previous example, the autonomy corresponding to 5.5 is:

$[(5.5-1) / 6] \times (100-5) + 5 = 76$ (rounded to the nearest whole number)

This method, although imperfect, allows you to make approximations until more data becomes available over time.

3. Develop an R&D project with the physical characteristics calculated above. This is done in cooperation with the R&D department as explained below.

4. Introduce a new brand or modifying an existing one. Completed R&D projects can be used to reposition existing brands by modifying the physical characteristics that are the basis of consumers' perceptions. They can also be used to introduce new brands. In both cases, a coherent advertising campaign will have to be implemented at the same time to inform consumers about these changes.

Note that this process will take at least one period.

7.5 Research & Development

The marketing department (you) may ask the R&D department to develop specific projects in order to improve existing products or to introduce new ones. The R&D department of the firm works for all the divisions, including yours, and operates as a profit center. Up to ten R&D projects may be ordered each period for the two markets, five Sonite projects and five Vodite projects. Over the course of the simulation, a maximum of thirty Sonite and thirty Vodite projects can be developed.

In the past, each firm has successfully completed two R&D projects on which the brands marketed in Period 0 are based. The project name starts with the letter *P* followed by the corresponding brand name. For instance, the R&D project corresponding to the existing brand *SAMA* was called *PSAMA*. To order a new project, the marketing department must specify the following information:

- project name;

- technical specifications of the desired product;

- target manufacturing unit cost;

- allocated development budget.

Project name

The names of R&D projects are made up of five characters. The first letter is always a *P* for project. The second letter identifies the type of product being developed, *S* for Sonite and *V* for Vodite. The firm can freely choose the last three characters.

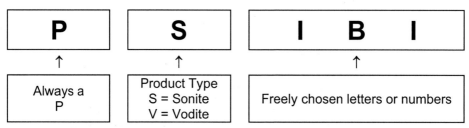

The name of a completed project can never be reused for a new project, even if it is a minor modification of the older project.

Technical specifications

The marketing department must provide the physical characteristics of the desired product. Each of the five attributes must be specified, and the levels must be within the feasible range. For instance, a Sonite project must include specifications for Weight, Design, Volume, Maximum Frequency and Power. Section 7.4 explains how to estimate the physical characteristics for product development.

Target manufacturing unit cost

The Marketing department must also provide the target manufacturing unit cost of the desired product. Because this cost decreases over time with experience and volume of production, you initially need to specify the transfer cost of the first 100,000 units of the new product. This cost is called the *Base cost*.

Base costs have no upper limit. If you indicate a high base cost, the R&D department will have more flexibility in finding the appropriate materials and manufacturing processes. As a consequence, the project is easier to develop, and is less expensive in terms of the total development budget.

The lower limit of the base cost for a given project depends on its technical specifications: the more sophisticated a product is, the higher the minimum base cost will be. High levels of design, maximum frequency, power and autonomy increase the base cost. Similarly, low levels of weight, diameter, and volume increase the base cost. This is understandable since a small, light and powerful Sonite is more complex than a big, heavy and low power Sonite.

There are many ways to estimate the base cost of a product.

- One solution is to start from the *ideal* price of the targeted segment, i.e. the price that consumers in this segment are willing to pay for a product fitting their needs. The base cost is then obtained by subtracting the average distributors' margin, plus the minimum margin that will make the future product economically attractive for you to market. This cost will be higher than the minimum one in many cases, but at least, this method provides the highest base cost economically achievable.

- Another method is to request that the R&D department develop the project at the minimum base cost. This solution is highly attractive in terms of margins, but may be more expensive overall since the development budget is likely to be much higher than the one required with the previous solution.

- A third procedure is to do an on-line query or a feasibility study, as explained in section 6.8. On-line queries and feasibility studies provide an estimate of the base cost and of the required development budget. On-line queries are free of charge and provide results instantaneously but they generally overestimate budget requirements. Feasibility studies cost $100,000 and take one period to complete but give fairly accurate results.

R&D expenditures

An R&D project includes the research work necessary to develop a prototype of the desired product, and the development work necessary to find potential suppliers and set up manufacturing processes. Your department must allocate a budget to each project to cover these R&D expenses. When the project is completed, the production department is ready to produce the first units of the product, at the transfer cost specified in the R&D report, assuming a first production batch of 100,000 units.

The budget required for the completion of a project is a function of several parameters. The budget depends on the requested physical characteristics: the more sophisticated the future product, the higher the budget. It also depends on the experience of the firm with comparable products, i.e. on the number of projects completed in the past with similar characteristics. Finally, the development budget depends on the base cost requested, as explained in the previous section. Note that the R&D department is managed as a profit center, and will not reimburse you if you allocate exceedingly high budgets.

Responses from the R&D department

All the R&D projects which the firm has worked on in the previous periods are listed in the R&D section of the company report. The report details completed and uncompleted projects, including the two projects which existed at the beginning of the simulation. A typical report is shown in Figure 15.

Let's use the following example to illustrate the possible responses from the R&D department. The table in Figure 30 summarizes the responses for a new project with identical physical characteristics but with four different requested levels of base cost and allocated budget.

Note that the *Minimum base cost* is the same in all cases because it only depends on the technical specifications. Similarly, the *Normal budget for completion* is the same in case A and B, or in cases C and D, because it depends on the technical specifications and on the requested base cost. The project is completed only in cases A and C. For the later one, the Marketing department could decide to immediately launch a cost reduction project, so as to complete a new project with the same physical characteristics and a base cost of $110.

Uncompleted R&D projects may be continued the following period, or may be suspended for one or several periods before being continued. If you choose to never continue the project, the budget allocated so far is lost. The technical characteristics of a continued project may not be changed from their original values. However the base cost may be changed without having to start a new project or sacrificing the money invested in the first project.

	Unit	Case A	Case B	Case C	Case D
Project specifications					
Weight	Kg	17	17	17	17
Design	Index	6	6	6	6
Volume	Dm3	85	85	85	85
Max Freq.	KHz	35	35	35	35
Power	W	70	70	70	70
Requested base cost	$	80	80	130	130
Allocated budget	K$	1 000	300	1 000	300
Parameters calculated by R&D at early stage of project					
Normal budget for completion	K$	800	800	550	550
Minimum Base Cost	$	110	110	110	110
Response from R&D at end of period					
Project successful	Y/N	Yes	No	Yes	No
Current base cost	$	110	110	130	130
Minimum base cost	$	110	110	110	110
Add. budget for completion	K$	-	500	-	250

Figure 30 – Interface with R&D department

Brand introduction, modification or withdrawal

R&D projects may be used as soon as they are completed to launch new brands or to modify existing ones. They may also be shelved for future use. Brand portfolio decisions are summarized below and are detailed in section 6.4.

A new brand is introduced on the market by entering a brand name which has not been used in the past. This brand name is completely independent of the code used for the R&D project. An existing brand is modified by keeping its current name and using the physical characteristics corresponding to a new completed project. Using a new brand name will facilitate the product's positioning, but the brand awareness will have to be completely built from scratch. Using an existing brand name makes its repositioning more difficult, since consumers are familiar with the brand at its previous position. However, as the awareness level is maintained, the brand's purchase intentions are likely to be higher than with a new brand.

The same product can be marketed under different names. The presence of multiple brands targeted at the same segment is a good strategy to build barriers to entry of new brands by competitors. A company may also market multiple brands based on the same project to different segments which are willing to pay different prices while having similar technical needs.

When a brand is modified, the Production department will immediately start producing the new version of the product. Lowering the cost of a brand is considered a brand modification. Obsolete inventories are sold by the Production department to a trading company at a fixed percentage of their value, usually 80%. This company will then export the old products outside the Markstrat Online world. Consequently, a loss of x% (the given percentage) of the inventory value is charged to the marketing department. The same rule applies if inventories remain when a brand is withdrawn from the market. For example, if the Marketing department decides to modify or withdraw brand SONO in Figure 14, the loss would be calculated as: 12 939 units x $146 x (100% – 80%) = K$ 377.8

8. Sample Decision Form

The following pages provide a sample decision form. As Markstrat Online includes a user-friendly windows-based decision support system, you will not have to fill in decision forms during the course. However, having a quick look at these two pages will allow you to anticipate the scope of all mandatory decisions.

The decisions you will have to key in are written in a script type like *115, 32 580, Flexibility, Yes,* etc.

BRAND MANAGEMENT – SONITE BRANDS

Sonite Brands Base R&D project		SEAL PSPR2	SEXY PSBU1	SEFA PSHI2		
Production planning	KU	200	150	200		
Inventory sold to trading company	KU	0	38	0		
Recommended retail price	$	400	350	450		
Advertising budget	K$	500	2 250	2 250		
Advertising research budget	K$	50	50	500		
	Buffs	5	100	0		
	Singles	5	0	0		
Targeted segments in %	Professionals	80	0	5		
	High earners	5	0	95		
	Others	5	0	0		
Perceptual Objectives						
Dimension 1		Eco.	Eco.	Perf.		
Objective 1	[1,7] or [-20,+20]	-5.0	5.0	4.0		
Dimension 2		Conv.	Perf..	Conv.		
Objective 2	[1,7] or [-20,+20]	1.0	15.0	-5.0		

BRAND MANAGEMENT – VODITE BRANDS

Sonite Brands Base R&D project		VETI PVETA				
Production planning	KU	100				
Inventory sold to trading company	KU	142				
Recommended retail price	$	1200				
Advertising budget	K$	2000				
Advertising research budget	K$	100				
	Innovators	0				
Targeted segments in %	Early adopters	100				
	Followers	0				
Perceptual Objectives Dimension 1		Eff.				
Objective 1	[1,7] or [-20,+20]	1.0				
Dimension 2		Felx.				
Objective 2	[1,7] or [-20,+20]	3.0				

SALES FORCE MANAGEMENT

Distribution Channels		Specialty stores	Depart. stores	Mass Merchants.
Number of salespeople		20	25	30
Sales force effort allocation by brand (%)	SEAL	33	45	47
	SEXY	14	8	10
	SEFA	19	27	43
	VETI	34	20	0
	TOTAL	100	100	100

SONITE R&D PROJECTS

Project	Allocated Budget K$	Product Characteristics					
		Weight Kg	Design Index	Volume Dm3	Max Freq. KHz	Power W	Base cost $
PSHI3	100	15	7	70	35	40	10
PSPR3	350	15	4	60	40	40	10

VODITE R&D PROJECTS

Project	Allocated Budget K$	Product Characteristics					
		Autonomy M	Max Freq. KHz	Diameter Mm	Design Index	Weight g	Base cost $
PVET1	500	60	10	50	5	50	10

MARKET RESEARCH STUDIES

Study	Market covered by study		
	All markets	Sonite	Vodite
Industry benchmarking	Yes	-	-
Consumer survey	-	Yes	Yes
Consumer panel	-	Yes	Yes
Distribution panel	-	Yes	Yes
Semantic scales	-	Yes	Yes
Multidimensional scaling	-	Yes	No
Market forecast	-	Yes	Yes
Competitive advertising	-	Yes	Yes
Competitive sales force	-	No	Yes
Advertising experiment	-	No	No
Sales force experiment	-	Yes	Yes
Conjoint analysis	-	No	No

9. Sample Annual Report

The following pages provide a sample annual report, composed of a Newsletter, a Company Report and Market Research Studies. To keep things simple, only Sonite studies have been included and the conjoint analysis results have not been given.

The annual report that you will receive in period 0 will be simpler. It will only include the Newsletter, the Company Report and a few Market Research Studies. In addition, your company will not have marketed any Vodite brands, making the report even shorter.

The data included in the following report is only for illustration purposes. It should not be used in making your decisions.

9.1 Newsletter

Newsletter – Stock market and KPIs

STOCK MARKET AND KEY PERFORMANCE INDICATORS

STOCK MARKET

Firm	Stock price index base 1000	Market capitalization K$	Net contribution (K$) Period 7	Cumulative
O	4 132	889 578	131 063	524 948
E	2 719	674 416	91 714	358 115
U	1 524	508 890	57 865	267 803
I	1 325	253 380	14 600	112 513
A	532	90 640	7 856	36 543

COMPANY KEY PERFORMANCE INDICATORS
(period 7 values)

	Unit	A	E	I	O	U
Market share						
Total	%$	4.2%	29.3%	12.1%	36.7%	17.7%
Sonite market	%$	7.8%	24.1%	22.3%	27.0%	18.8%
Vodite market	%$	0.0%	35.5%	0.0%	48.2%	16.3%
Retail sales						
Total	K$	48 280	333 214	138 150	417 289	201 369
Sonite market	K$	48 280	149 388	138 150	167 849	116 949
Vodite market	K$	0	183 825	0	249 441	84 421
Contribution						
Before marketing	K$	12 565	116 064	24 485	155 412	73 014
After marketing	K$	8 421	92 832	17 731	135 156	58 585
Net	K$	7 856	91 714	14 600	131 063	57 865
Cumulative net	K$	36 543	358 115	112 513	524 948	267 803
Shareholder value						
Stock price index	Base 1000	532	2 719	1 325	4 132	1 524
Market capitalization	K$	90 640	674 416	253 380	889 578	508 890
Current return on investment	Ratio	1.67	3.77	1.48	5.38	3.82
Cumulative return on investment	Ratio	0.67	3.45	1.92	4.33	3.52

COMPANY KEY PERFORMANCE INDICATORS
(% change from period 6 to period 7)

	A	E	I	O	U
Market share					
Total	-1.0%	-0.5%	-2.6%	-3.2%	10.9%
Sonite market	18.5%	2.6%	16.6%	-0.9%	-20.2%
Vodite market	-	-12.7%	-	-16.6%	926.4%
Retail sales					
Total	17.5%	18.1%	15.6%	15.0%	31.6%
Sonite market	17.5%	1.8%	15.6%	-1.7%	-20.8%
Vodite market	-	35.8%	-	29.7%	1496.0%
Contribution					
Before marketing	382.3%	25.1%	-39.6%	25.1%	33.6%
After marketing	-320.6%	17.6%	-48.3%	28.9%	34.0%
Net	-240.7%	23.6%	-55.0%	28.0%	39.7%
Cumulative net	27.4%	34.4%	14.9%	33.3%	27.6%
Shareholder value					
Stock price index	14.3%	19.3%	-3.9%	5.0%	1.4%
Market capitalization	14.3%	19.3%	-3.9%	5.0%	1.4%
Current return on investment	-344.6%	-5.6%	-62.9%	14.8%	22.0%
Cumulative return on investment	16.4%	2.8%	-4.5%	6.5%	2.2%

Newsletter – Economic variables and costs

ECONOMIC VARIABLES AND COSTS

ECONOMIC VARIABLES

	Unit	Actual value Period 7	Forecast value Period 8	%change
GNP growth rates	%	2.0%	2.0%	0.0%
Inflation rate	%	2.0%	2.0%	0.0%
Production				
Inventory holding cost per annum	% transf. cost	8.0%	8.0%	0.0%
Loss incurred for inventory disposal	transf. cost	20.0%	20.0%	0.0%
Sales force				
Salesperson operating cost	$	24 839	25 336	2.0%
Salesperson hiring and training cost	$	3 726	3 800	2.0%
Salesperson firing cost	$	6 210	6 334	2.0%

COST OF MARKET RESEARCH STUDIES NEXT PERIOD
(all numbers in K$)

Study	Market covered by study		
	All markets	Sonite	Vodite
Industry benchmarking	38		
Consumer survey		76	51
Consumer panel		127	89
Distribution panel		76	63
Semantic scales		13	13
Multidimensional scaling		44	44
Market forecast		25	25
Competitive advertising		38	38
Competitive sales force		19	19
Advertising experiment		32	32
Sales force experiment		44	44
Conjoint analysis		44	44
Total market	38	538	462
Total if all studies ordered	1 038		

Newsletter – Information on Sonite market

INFORMATION ON SONITE MARKET

CHARACTERISTICS OF MARKETED SONITE BRANDS

Firm	Brand	New or modified	Physical characteristics					Base cost ($)	Retail price ($)
			Weight (Kg)	Design (Index)	Volume (Dm3)	Max Freq (KHz)	Power (W)		
A	SAMA	No	17	6	92	23	32	105	204
	SALT	No	17	7	75	35	65	176	279
	SAND	No	14	4	50	40	85	198	514
E	SEMI	Modified	14	5	50	40	80	197	565
	SELF	No	14	5	50	40	80	197	550
	SEBU	No	13	7	40	40	75	197	420
	SERT	No	13	7	50	30	55	198	478
I	SIBI	Modified	19	8	60	36	66	187	271
	SIPE	Cost impr.	20	7	70	15	30	91	203
	SICK	Modified	19	8	60	36	66	187	290
O	SOLD	No	14	7	38	30	55	165	460
	SONO	No	14	5	50	40	77	192	545
	SODU	No	16	7	75	34	54	142	267
	SODE	No	15	7	40	38	77	205	417
U	SUSI	No	17	6	88	23	30	94	220
	SULI	No	14	5	50	40	77	190	540
	SUBF	New	17	4	65	35	70	146	325

INFORMATION ON SONITE MARKET - SALES AND MARKET SHARES

Firm	Brand	Volume sold				Retail sales			
		Period 6	Period 7	Change	Share	Period 6	Period 7	Change	Share
		U	U	%	%U	K$	K$	%	%$
A	SAMA	107 875	243 583	125.8%	12.4%	20 594	47 496	130.6%	7.7%
	SALT	42 754	2 543	-94.1%	0.1%	11 295	685	-93.9%	0.1%
	SAND	18 228	197	-98.9%	0.0%	9 208	99	-98.9%	0.0%
E	SEMI	64 933	104 317	60.7%	5.3%	35 102	57 684	64.3%	9.3%
	SELF	50 726	1 017	-98.0%	0.1%	27 440	545	-98.0%	0.1%
	SEBU	87 049	88 456	1.6%	4.5%	36 365	36 887	1.4%	5.9%
	SERT	100 949	114 720	13.6%	5.8%	47 893	54 271	13.3%	8.7%
I	SIBI	319 851	411 600	28.7%	20.9%	93 636	109 007	16.4%	17.6%
	SIPE	55 200	114 000	106.5%	5.8%	13 045	21 940	68.2%	3.5%
	SICK	45 096	25 410	-43.7%	1.3%	12 826	7 203	-43.8%	1.2%
O	SOLD	134 875	132 025	-2.1%	6.7%	65 595	60 002	-8.5%	9.7%
	SONO	72 077	83 061	15.2%	4.2%	38 233	44 427	16.2%	7.2%
	SODU	212 826	177 174	-16.8%	9.0%	55 569	46 249	-16.8%	7.5%
	SODE	27 249	41 378	51.9%	2.1%	11 315	17 172	51.8%	2.8%
U	SUSI	402 680	335 890	-16.6%	17.1%	86 052	70 076	-18.6%	11.3%
	SULI	115 973	86 803	-25.2%	4.4%	61 660	46 047	-25.3%	7.4%
	SUBF	0	2 601	-	0.1%	0	825	-	0.1%
Total Sonite market		1 858 341	1 964 777	5.7%	100.0%	625 825	620 617	-0.8%	100.0%

Newsletter – Information on Vodite market

INFORMATION ON VODITE MARKET

CHARACTERISTICS OF MARKETED VODITE BRANDS

Firm	Brand	New or modified	Physical characteristics					Base cost ($)	Retail price ($)
			Autonomy (M)	Max Freq (KHz)	Diameter (Mm)	Design (Index)	Weight (g)		
E	VENI	No	70	13	70	7	60	275	1 090
	VEDI	No	70	13	70	7	60	275	900
	VECI	No	53	12	56	7	58	303	730
O	VOOM	No	78	14	68	7	70	253	810
	VOOT	Cost impr.	57	12	55	7	70	239	690
	VOOZ	No	78	14	68	7	70	253	1 000
U	VUDA	No	60	12	55	7	60	287	730

INFORMATION ON VODITE MARKET - SALES AND MARKET SHARES

Firm	Brand	Volume sold				Retail sales			
		Period 6 U	Period 7 U	Change %	Share %U	Period 6 K$	Period 7 K$	Change %	Share %$
E	VENI	22 699	8 521	-62.5%	1.2%	24 612	9 240	-62.5%	1.8%
	VEDI	33 243	51 574	55.1%	7.2%	32 177	45 778	42.3%	8.8%
	VECI	110 783	184 672	66.7%	25.6%	78 594	128 807	63.9%	24.9%
O	VOOM	61 772	77 319	25.2%	10.7%	52 739	61 740	17.1%	11.9%
	VOOT	170 400	263 128	54.4%	36.5%	119 158	173 250	45.4%	33.5%
	VOOZ	18 540	14 460	-22.0%	2.0%	20 369	14 450	-29.1%	2.8%
U	VUDA	7 314	121 325	1558.9%	16.8%	5 290	84 421	1496.0%	16.3%
Total Vodite market		424 750	721 000	69.7%	100.0%	332 938	517 687	55.5%	100.0%

9.2 Company Report

Company Report – Company results

COMPANY RESULTS

COMPANY SCORECARD

	Unit	Annual results			Evolution since P0	
		Period 6	Period 7	%change	Ratio P7/P0	Average growth
Market share						
Total	%$	37.9%	36.7%	-3.2%	× 1.60	6.9%
Sonite market	%$	27.3%	27.0%	-0.9%	× 1.18	2.4%
Vodite market	%$	57.7%	48.2%	-16.6%	-	-
Retail sales						
Total	K$	362 977	417 289	15.0%	× 6.26	30.0%
Sonite market	K$	170 711	167 849	-1.7%	× 2.52	14.1%
Vodite market	K$	192 266	249 441	29.7%	-	-
Contribution						
Before marketing	K$	124 263	155 412	25.1%	× 9.65	38.2%
After marketing	K$	104 857	135 156	28.9%	× 12.43	43.3%
Net	K$	102 418	131 063	28.0%	× 12.33	43.2%
Cumulative net	K$	393 885	524 948	33.3%	× 49.38	74.6%
Shareholder value						
Stock price index	Base 1000	3 936	4 132	5.0%	× 4.13	22.5%
Current return on investment	Ratio	4.69	5.38	14.8%	× 2.77	15.7%
Cumulative return on investment	Ratio	4.06	4.33	6.5%	× 2.23	12.1%

COMPANY PERFORMANCE

	Unit	Total	Sonite market	Vodite market
Sales				
Units sold	U	788 546	433 639	354 908
Average retail price	$	529	387	703
Average selling price	$	350	253	468
Revenues	K$	275 610	109 629	165 982
Production				
Units produced	U	747 100	371 400	375 700
Cost of goods sold	K$	-119 740	-53 048	-66 692
Inventory holding cost	K$	-458	-152	-306
Inventory disposal loss	K$	0	0	0
Contribution before marketing	K$	155 412	56 429	98 983
Marketing				
Advertising expenditures	K$	-12 204	-6 697	-5 507
Advertising research expenditures	K$	-1 657	-1 074	-583
Sales force	K$	-6 395	-4 210	-2 185
Contribution after marketing	K$	135 156	44 448	90 708
Other expenses				
Market research studies	K$	-1 018	-528	-453
Research and development	K$	-3 075	-1 975	-1 100
Interest paid	K$	0		
Exceptional cost or profit	K$	0		
Net contribution	K$	131 063		
Next period budget	K$	24 850		

Company Report – Instructor & simulation messages

INSTRUCTOR AND SIMULATION MESSAGES

Messages
Despite all the efforts made by the Production department, they were not able to fullfill all the orders for brand SOLD this period. As a consequence, some potential sales of this brand have been lost.
Despite all the efforts made by the Production department, they were not able to fullfill all the orders for brand SODU this period. As a consequence, some potential sales of this brand have been lost.
Despite all the efforts made by the Production department, they were not able to fullfill all the orders for brand VOOZ this period. As a consequence, some potential sales of this brand have been lost.

Company Report – Brand results

BRAND RESULTS

CONTRIBUTION BY BRAND

Sonite Brands	Unit	Total	SOLD	SONO	SODU	SODE
Base R&D project			PSOL2	PSON2	PSOSI	PSOBU
Sales						
Units sold	U	433 639	132 025	83 061	177 174	41 378
Average retail price	$	387	454	535	261	415
Average selling price	$	253	304	343	171	256
Revenues	K$	109 629	40 147	28 516	30 368	10 597
Production						
Units produced	U	371 400	132 000	96 000	102 000	41 400
Current unit transfer cost	$	-	129	146	84	219
Average unit transfer cost	$	122	129	146	84	220
Cost of goods sold	K$	-53 048	-16 991	-12 087	-14 885	-9 085
Units in inventory	U	13 012	0	12 939	0	73
Inventory holding cost	K$	-152	0	-151	0	-1
Inventory disposal loss	K$	0	0	0	0	0
Contribution before marketing	K$	56 429	23 156	16 278	15 484	1 511
Marketing						
Advertising expenditures	K$	-6 697	-2 001	-1 496	-2 005	-1 195
Advertising research expenditures	K$	-1 074	-299	-204	-326	-245
Sales force	K$	-4 210	-1 814	-1 032	-960	-404
Contribution after marketing	K$	44 448	19 042	13 546	12 192	-333

CONTRIBUTION BY BRAND

Vodite Brands	Unit	Total	VOOM	VOOT	VOOZ
Base R&D project			PVOOM	PVOT3	PVOOM
Sales					
Units sold	U	354 908	77 319	263 128	14 460
Average retail price	$	703	799	658	999
Average selling price	$	468	507	448	611
Revenues	K$	165 982	39 185	117 965	8 831
Production					
Units produced	U	375 700	77 300	284 000	14 400
Current unit transfer cost	$	-	201	183	201
Average unit transfer cost	$	188	201	183	201
Cost of goods sold	K$	-66 692	-15 573	-48 205	-2 914
Units in inventory	U	20 881	9	20 872	0
Inventory holding cost	K$	-306	0	-306	0
Inventory disposal loss	K$	0	0	0	0
Contribution before marketing	K$	98 983	23 612	69 454	5 917
Marketing					
Advertising expenditures	K$	-5 507	-1 702	-3 203	-602
Advertising research expenditures	K$	-583	-168	-317	-98
Sales force	K$	-2 185	-613	-1 336	-235
Contribution after marketing	K$	90 708	21 128	64 598	4 982

MARKET SHARES AND DISTRIBUTION COVERAGE

Sonite Brands	Unit	Total	SOLD	SONO	SODU	SODE
Market shares	%U	22.1%	6.7%	4.2%	9.0%	2.1%
	%$	27.0%	9.7%	7.2%	7.5%	2.8%
Distribution coverage in %						
Specialty stores (27 273 outlets)	%		44.9%	48.3%	45.2%	34.6%
Depart. stores (6 638 outlets)	%		53.7%	30.6%	35.6%	13.4%
Mass Merchandis. (12 603 outlets	%		27.5%	19.9%	22.1%	5.4%

Company Report – Brand results (cont'd)

MARKET SHARES AND DISTRIBUTION COVERAGE

Vodite Brands	Unit	Total	VOOM	VOOT	VOOZ
Market shares	%U	49.2%	10.7%	36.5%	2.0%
	%S	48.2%	11.9%	33.5%	2.8%
Distribution coverage in %					
Specialty stores (27 273 outlets)	%		41.3%	40.3%	28.9%
Depart. stores (6 638 outlets)	%		29.5%	58.7%	12.5%
Mass Merchandis. (12 603 outlets	%		23.3%	62.6%	0.2%

Company Report – Research & development results

RESEARCH & DEVELOPMENT RESULTS

SONITE R&D PROJECTS

Name	Physical Characteristics					Base Cost $		Allocated Budget K$	
	Weight (Kg)	Design (Index)	Volume (Dm3)	Max Freq (KHz)	Power (W)	Current	Minimum realistic	Cumulative	Req. for completion
PSOLD	13	7	45	30	75	203	166	1 500	Avail. in P-1
PSONO	16	4	75	48	88	224	176	2 000	Avail. in P-1
PSOPR	16	5	75	40	75	176	158	963	Avail. in P2
PSOSI	16	7	75	34	54	142	134	1 050	Avail. in P2
PSON2	14	5	50	40	77	192	166	810	Avail. in P4
PSODU	16	7	75	36	63	148	147	940	Avail. in P6
PSOL2	14	7	38	30	55	165	141	756	Avail. in P5
PSOBU	15	7	40	38	77	205	175	918	Avail. in P5
PSON3	14	6	50	40	80	174	174	100	990
PSOD2*	16	7	40	35	77	205	173	550	Avail. in P7
PSOU2*	16	7	78	43	54	148	140	925	Avail. in P7
PSOL3*	14	7	38	25	55	165	138	500	Avail. in P7

(*) Projects written in bold font have just been completed this period.

VODITE R&D PROJECTS

Name	Physical Characteristics					Base Cost $		Allocated Budget K$	
	Autonomy (M)	Max Freq (KHz)	Diameter (Mm)	Design (Index)	Weight (g)	Current	Minimum realistic	Cumulative	Req. for completion
PVARI	51	12	68	7	70	223	223	7 260	Avail. in P3
PVOOM	78	14	68	7	70	253	253	2 943	Avail. in P4
PVOOT	67	7	70	7	70	217	217	100	1 900
PVOT2	57	12	55	7	70	285	239	1 710	Avail. in P5
PVOT3	57	12	55	7	70	239	239	500	Avail. in P6
PVOT4	60	12	53	7	60	261	261	1 000	790
PVOT5	60	12	53	7	60	261	261	100	1 690

(*) Projects written in bold font have just been completed this period.

Company Report – Cumulative results

CUMULATIVE RESULTS

CUMULATIVE BRAND RESULTS

Brand	Results since period	Sales			Production		Marketing		Contrib. after mktg.
		Units sold	Retail sales	Revenues	Cost of goods sold	Inventory costs	Advertising	Sales force	
		KU	K$	K$	K$	K$	K$	K$	K$
SOLD	0	1 238	632 171	421 052	154 939	1 243	15 785	10 774	238 312
SONO	0	544	254 832	163 065	89 758	2 223	12 482	6 035	52 568
SODU	3	876	241 261	158 672	80 976	630	10 019	4 111	62 936
SODE	5	77	31 710	19 591	17 560	725	4 420	1 295	-4 409
VOOM	4	215	191 467	121 769	47 640	4	6 640	2 978	64 508
VOOT	4	497	353 488	239 344	102 454	306	11 515	3 760	121 309
VOOZ	5	49	51 814	32 047	10 792	1	3 360	1 078	16 816
Total Sonite		2 735	1 159 974	762 380	343 233	4 821	42 705	22 214	349 407
Total Vodite		760	596 769	393 161	160 886	311	21 514	7 816	202 633
all markets		3 495	1 756 743	1 155 541	504 119	5 132	64 220	30 030	552 040

CUMULATIVE COMPANY PERFORMANCE

	Unit	Total	Sonite market	Vodite market
Sales				
Units sold	KU	3 495	2 735	760
Retail sales	K$	1 756 743	1 159 974	596 769
Revenues	K$	1 155 541	762 380	393 161
Production				
Cost of goods sold	K$	-504 119	-343 233	-160 886
Inventory holding and disposal cost	K$	-5 132	-4 821	-311
Marketing				
Total advertising expenditures	K$	-64 220	-42 705	-21 514
Sales force expenditures	K$	-30 030	-22 214	-7 816
Contribution after marketing	K$	552 040	349 407	202 633
Other expenses				
Market research studies	K$	-5 967	-3 556	-2 173
Research and development	K$	-21 125	-7 512	-13 613
Interest paid	K$	0		
Exceptional cost or profit	K$	0		
Net contribution	K$	524 948		

Company Report – Decisions summary

DECISION SUMMARY

DECISION SUMMARY - BRAND MANAGEMENT

Sonite Brands		SOLD	SONO	SODU	SODE
Base R&D project		PSOL2	PSON2	PSOSI	PSOBU
Production planning	KU	110	120	85	50
Inventory sold to trading company	KU	0	0	0	0
Recommended retail price	$	460	545	267	417
Advertising budget	K$	2 001	1 496	2 005	1 195
Advertising research budget	K$	299	204	326	245
	Buffs	0	0	0	100
	Singles	0	0	100	0
Targeted segments in %	Professionals	0	100	0	0
	High earners	100	0	0	0
	Others	0	0	0	0
Perceptual Objectives					
Dimension 1		Performance	Convenience	Convenience	Convenience
Objective 1	[1,7] or [-20,+20]	1.0	-4.0	3.0	4.0
Dimension 2		Convenience	Performance	None	None
Objective 2	[1,7] or [-20,+20]	4.0	13.0	-	-

DECISION SUMMARY - BRAND MANAGEMENT

Vodite Brands		VOOM	VOOT	VOOZ
Base R&D project		PVOOM	PVOT3	PVOOM
Production planning	KU	91	355	12
Inventory sold to trading company	KU	0	0	0
Recommended retail price	$	810	690	1 000
Advertising budget	K$	1 702	3 203	602
Advertising research budget	K$	168	317	98
	Innovators	0	0	100
Targeted segments in %	Early Adopters	100	0	0
	Followers	0	100	0
Perceptual Objectives				
Dimension 1		Economy	Economy	Efficacy
Objective 1	[1,7] or [-20,+20]	-5.0	-1.0	7.0
Dimension 2		Efficacy	Flexibility	Flexibility
Objective 2	[1,7] or [-20,+20]	5.0	1.0	4.0

DECISION SUMMARY - SALES FORCE MANAGEMENT

Distribution Channels	Specialty stores	Depart. stores	Mass Merchandis.
Number of salespeople	95	93	69
Sales force effort allocation by brand (%)			
SOLD	17	41	27
SONO	21	12	15
SODU	17	13	15
SODE	11	4	3
VOOM	14	7	7
VOOT	12	21	33
VOOZ	8	2	0
TOTAL	100	100	100

Company Report – Decisions summary (cont'd)

DECISION SUMMARY - SONITE R&D PROJECTS

Project	Expenditures	Product Characteristics					
		Weight	Design Index	Volume	Max Freq	Power	Base cost
	K$	Kg	Index	Dm3	KHz	W	$
PSOD2	550	16	7	40	35	77	201
PSOU2	925	16	7	78	43	54	145
PSOL3	500	14	7	38	25	55	162

DECISION SUMMARY - VODITE R&D PROJECTS

Project	Expenditures	Product Characteristics					
		Autonomy	Max Freq	Diameter	Design	Weight	Base cost
	K$	M	KHz	Mm	Index	g	$
PVOT4	1 000	60	12	53	7	60	234
PVOT5	100	60	12	53	7	60	10

DECISION SUMMARY - MARKET RESEARCH STUDIES

Study	Market covered by study		
	All markets	Sonite	Vodite
Industry benchmarking	Yes	-	-
Consumer survey	-	Yes	Yes
Consumer panel	-	Yes	Yes
Distribution panel	-	Yes	Yes
Semantic scales	-	Yes	Yes
Multidimensional scaling	-	Yes	Yes
Market forecast	-	Yes	Yes
Competitive advertising	-	Yes	Yes
Competitive sales force	-	Yes	Yes
Advertising experiment	-	Yes	Yes
Sales force experiment	-	Yes	Yes
Conjoint analysis	-	Yes	Yes

DECISION SUMMARY - LOAN AND BUDGET MODIFICATION

	Unit	
Corporate finance department		
Increase in budget	K$	0
Decrease in budget	K$	0
Bank		
Capital borrowed	K$	0
Duration in number of periods		
Interest rate	%	

9.3 Market Research Studies

Market Research Studies – Industry benchmarking

INDUSTRY BENCHMARKING

BENCHMARKING - ESTIMATED OVERALL PERFORMANCE

	Unit	A	E	I	O	U
Sales						
Retail sales	K$	48 280	333 214	138 150	417 289	201 369
Revenues	K$	32 992	219 007	91 618	275 610	136 305
Production						
Cost of goods sold	K$	-19 476	-100 494	-66 427	-119 740	-62 054
Inventory holding cost	K$	-950	-1 666	-2	-458	-1 237
Inventory disposal loss	K$	0	-783	-704	0	0
Contribution before marketing	K$	12 565	116 064	24 485	155 412	73 014
Marketing						
Advertising expenditures	K$	-1 696	-14 406	-3 710	-12 204	-9 296
Advertising research expenditures	K$	-89	-1 425	-440	-1 657	-919
Sales force	K$	-2 360	-7 401	-2 604	-6 395	-4 214
Contribution after marketing	K$	8 421	92 832	17 731	135 156	58 585
Other expenses						
Market research studies	K$	-565	-1 018	-621	-1 018	-720
Research and development	K$	0	-100	-2 510	-3 075	0
Interest paid	K$	0	0	0	0	0
Exceptional cost or profit	K$	0	0	0	0	0
Net contribution	K$	7 856	91 714	14 600	131 063	57 865
Next period budget	K$	8 700	24 850	8 700	24 850	23 150

BENCHMARKING - ESTIMATED PERFORMANCE IN SONITE MARKET

	Unit	A	E	I	O	U
Sales						
Retail sales	K$	48 280	149 388	138 150	167 849	116 949
Revenues	K$	32 992	96 890	91 618	109 629	78 565
Production						
Cost of goods sold	K$	-19 476	-43 935	-66 427	-53 048	-32 127
Inventory holding cost	K$	-950	-490	-2	-152	-618
Inventory disposal loss	K$	0	-783	-704	0	0
Contribution before marketing	K$	12 565	51 682	24 485	56 429	45 819
Marketing						
Advertising expenditures	K$	-1 696	-7 211	-3 710	-6 697	-6 006
Advertising research expenditures	K$	-89	-713	-440	-1 074	-594
Sales force	K$	-2 360	-4 534	-2 604	-4 210	-3 563
Contribution after marketing	K$	8 421	39 224	17 731	44 448	35 657

BENCHMARKING - ESTIMATED PERFORMANCE IN VODITE MARKET

	Unit	A	E	I	O	U
Sales						
Retail sales	K$	0	183 825	0	249 441	84 421
Revenues	K$	0	122 117	0	165 982	57 740
Production						
Cost of goods sold	K$	0	-56 559	0	-66 692	-29 926
Inventory holding cost	K$	0	-1 176	0	-306	-619
Inventory disposal loss	K$	0	0	0	0	0
Contribution before marketing	K$	0	64 382	0	98 983	27 195
Marketing						
Advertising expenditures	K$	0	-7 195	0	-5 507	-3 290
Advertising research expenditures	K$	0	-712	0	-583	-325
Sales force	K$	0	-2 867	0	-2 185	-651
Contribution after marketing	K$	0	53 608	0	90 708	22 929

Market Research Studies – Consumer survey

CONSUMER SURVEY - SONITE MARKET

CONSUMER SURVEY - BRAND AWARENESS BY SEGMENT

Firm	Brand	Buffs	Singles	Pros	HiEarners	Others	Total
A	SAMA	46.3%	52.5%	44.9%	47.9%	61.7%	53.8%
	SALT	44.4%	54.8%	41.1%	43.4%	33.6%	43.2%
	SAND	18.4%	14.8%	43.5%	28.6%	13.4%	20.1%
E	SEMI	57.1%	49.3%	76.3%	57.0%	39.4%	50.9%
	SELF	41.5%	34.8%	52.6%	41.1%	23.5%	34.4%
	SEBU	70.6%	24.9%	30.9%	27.8%	19.3%	27.2%
	SERT	32.1%	25.1%	31.0%	67.9%	23.7%	31.2%
I	SIBI	50.5%	66.1%	46.5%	47.7%	37.5%	49.8%
	SIPE	24.8%	21.7%	26.6%	25.7%	48.5%	32.7%
	SICK	22.7%	45.1%	22.0%	20.7%	15.9%	26.9%
O	SOLD	60.6%	55.7%	59.4%	77.7%	49.7%	57.1%
	SONO	53.3%	43.1%	73.4%	45.6%	34.7%	45.2%
	SODU	34.7%	58.5%	33.6%	31.5%	26.6%	38.7%
	SODE	57.9%	11.9%	16.9%	14.3%	9.6%	15.2%
U	SUSI	42.0%	48.6%	46.3%	47.8%	65.8%	53.9%
	SULI	59.6%	51.0%	77.4%	59.6%	41.7%	52.9%
	SUBF	11.7%	19.7%	11.0%	10.3%	8.0%	12.6%

CONSUMER SURVEY - PURCHASE INTENTIONS

Firm	Brand	Buffs	Singles	Pros	HiEarners	Others	Total
A	SAMA	0.1%	0.4%	0.0%	0.1%	20.9%	7.4%
	SALT	0.3%	4.1%	0.1%	0.3%	1.1%	1.8%
	SAND	0.2%	0.0%	3.7%	0.3%	0.1%	0.6%
E	SEMI	0.8%	0.1%	30.0%	0.7%	0.2%	4.4%
	SELF	0.4%	0.1%	8.7%	0.4%	0.1%	1.4%
	SEBU	54.1%	0.2%	0.3%	0.6%	0.1%	4.1%
	SERT	0.5%	0.1%	0.3%	31.6%	0.1%	3.7%
I	SIBI	0.3%	46.5%	0.1%	0.2%	1.1%	15.8%
	SIPE	0.1%	0.2%	0.0%	0.1%	44.0%	15.3%
	SICK	0.2%	6.0%	0.0%	0.1%	0.7%	2.2%
O	SOLD	1.2%	0.2%	0.5%	63.9%	0.3%	7.5%
	SONO	0.8%	0.1%	28.9%	0.5%	0.1%	4.2%
	SODU	0.2%	41.2%	0.0%	0.1%	0.8%	13.9%
	SODE	39.8%	0.1%	0.2%	0.3%	0.1%	3.0%
U	SUSI	0.1%	0.3%	0.0%	0.1%	30.0%	10.5%
	SULI	0.8%	0.1%	27.2%	0.7%	0.2%	4.0%
	SUBF	0.1%	0.3%	0.0%	0.0%	0.1%	0.1%
Total		100.0%	100.0%	100.0%	100.0%	100.0%	100.0%

CONSUMER SURVEY - SHOPPING HABITS

Segment	Specialty stores	Depart. stores	Mass Merchandis.	Total
Buffs	59.1%	22.3%	18.6%	100.0%
Singles	34.5%	34.5%	30.9%	100.0%
Professionals	41.8%	27.3%	30.9%	100.0%
High earners	30.9%	50.0%	19.1%	100.0%
Others	14.5%	34.5%	51.0%	100.0%
Total	29.5%	34.6%	35.8%	100.0%

Market Research Studies – Consumer panel

CONSUMER PANEL - SONITE MARKET

CONSUMER PANEL - MARKET SHARES BASED ON UNIT SALES

Firm	Brand	Buffs	Singles	Pros	HiEarners	Others	Total
A	SAMA	0.2%	0.6%	0.1%	0.2%	33.7%	12.4%
	SALT	0.0%	0.3%	0.0%	0.0%	0.1%	0.1%
	SAND	0.0%	0.0%	0.1%	0.0%	0.0%	0.0%
E	SEMI	1.1%	0.2%	37.4%	0.7%	0.2%	5.3%
	SELF	0.0%	0.0%	0.3%	0.0%	0.0%	0.1%
	SEBU	63.7%	0.2%	0.3%	0.5%	0.1%	4.5%
	SERT	0.8%	0.1%	0.4%	45.1%	0.2%	5.8%
I	SIBI	0.5%	65.3%	0.1%	0.3%	1.3%	20.9%
	SIPE	0.0%	0.1%	0.0%	0.0%	16.0%	5.8%
	SICK	0.1%	3.7%	0.0%	0.1%	0.3%	1.3%
O	SOLD	1.1%	0.2%	0.4%	51.6%	0.3%	6.7%
	SONO	0.9%	0.1%	29.9%	0.5%	0.1%	4.2%
	SODU	0.2%	28.2%	0.0%	0.1%	0.5%	9.0%
	SODE	30.2%	0.0%	0.1%	0.1%	0.0%	2.1%
U	SUSI	0.1%	0.5%	0.0%	0.2%	46.9%	17.1%
	SULI	1.0%	0.2%	30.9%	0.6%	0.1%	4.4%
	SUBF	0.1%	0.3%	0.0%	0.0%	0.1%	0.1%
Total		100.0%	100.0%	100.0%	100.0%	100.0%	100.0%
Total sales (U)		133 345	613 947	264 877	244 977	707 630	1 964 777
Total sales (% Total)		6.8%	31.2%	13.5%	12.5%	36.0%	100.0%

Market Research Studies – Distribution panel

DISTRIBUTION PANEL - SONITE MARKET

DISTRIBUTION PANEL - MARKET SHARES BASED ON UNIT SALES

Firm	Brand	Specialty stores	Depart. stores	Mass Merchandis.	Total
A	SAMA	5.7%	13.4%	18.9%	12.4%
	SALT	0.1%	0.1%	0.2%	0.1%
	SAND	0.0%	0.0%	0.0%	0.0%
E	SEMI	8.1%	3.9%	3.9%	5.3%
	SELF	0.1%	0.0%	0.0%	0.1%
	SEBU	10.3%	1.9%	1.1%	4.5%
	SERT	5.6%	9.0%	2.1%	5.8%
I	SIBI	25.4%	20.5%	16.4%	20.9%
	SIPE	1.7%	5.9%	10.4%	5.8%
	SICK	1.6%	1.3%	1.0%	1.3%
O	SOLD	6.1%	10.4%	2.8%	6.7%
	SONO	7.2%	2.8%	2.7%	4.2%
	SODU	11.3%	8.5%	6.9%	9.0%
	SODE	5.2%	0.7%	0.3%	2.1%
U	SUSI	4.1%	18.4%	30.5%	17.1%
	SULI	7.5%	3.0%	2.7%	4.4%
	SUBF	0.1%	0.2%	0.1%	0.1%
Total		100.0%	100.0%	100.0%	100.0%
Total sales (U)		662 603	732 176	569 998	1 964 777
Total sales (% Total)		33.7%	37.3%	29.0%	100.0%

DISTRIBUTION PANEL - DISTRIBUTION COVERAGE BY CHANNEL

Firm	Brand	Specialty stores	Depart. stores	Mass Merchandis.
A	SAMA	47.0%	51.0%	34.7%
	SALT	0.3%	0.3%	0.3%
	SAND	0.1%	0.1%	0.1%
E	SEMI	52.6%	42.1%	28.5%
	SELF	0.3%	0.2%	0.2%
	SEBU	51.7%	26.2%	13.5%
	SERT	45.2%	51.1%	22.4%
I	SIBI	41.3%	36.6%	21.1%
	SIPE	26.2%	41.5%	33.0%
	SICK	16.1%	13.8%	8.2%
O	SOLD	44.9%	53.7%	27.5%
	SONO	48.3%	30.6%	19.9%
	SODU	45.2%	36.6%	22.1%
	SODE	34.6%	13.4%	5.4%
U	SUSI	21.1%	47.5%	37.8%
	SULI	53.8%	35.2%	20.9%
	SUBF	24.4%	31.4%	15.5%
Total number of outlets		27 273	6 638	12 603

Market Research Studies – Semantic scales

SEMANTIC SCALES - SONITE MARKET

SEMANTIC SCALES - IDEAL VALUES (1 TO 7)

Segment	Weight	Design	Volume	Max Freq	Power	Price
Buffs	3.94	4.88	3.14	5.64	5.56	4.87
Singles	5.64	5.20	5.02	5.11	4.87	2.70
Pros	3.43	2.77	3.29	5.94	5.85	6.34
HiEarners	4.82	5.48	4.88	3.79	4.27	5.55
Others	5.24	4.05	6.02	3.47	2.71	2.05
Importance of characteristic (1)	1	4	2	3	6	10

(1) On a scale from 1 to 10 - 1 = Not important - 10 = Very important

SEMANTIC SCALES - BRAND PERCEPTIONS (1 TO 7)

Firm	Brand	Weight	Design	Volume	Max Freq	Power	Price
A	SAMA	5.47	3.03	6.05	3.00	2.61	2.12
	SALT	5.41	4.19	4.79	4.64	4.38	3.03
	SAND	3.52	1.86	3.41	5.64	5.99	5.99
E	SEMI	3.17	2.82	2.99	5.81	5.89	6.24
	SELF	3.59	2.04	2.82	5.99	5.96	6.27
	SEBU	2.71	4.60	2.44	5.78	5.55	4.83
	SERT	2.70	4.70	3.16	4.37	4.08	5.79
I	SIBI	6.45	5.66	4.00	5.04	4.69	2.65
	SIPE	6.50	4.27	4.86	2.24	2.71	2.06
	SICK	6.45	5.66	4.00	4.74	4.27	2.78
O	SOLD	3.26	4.60	2.35	4.36	4.19	5.58
	SONO	3.31	2.71	3.14	5.84	5.83	6.16
	SODU	4.68	4.92	5.20	5.16	4.68	2.61
	SODE	3.90	4.42	2.50	5.58	5.73	4.98
U	SUSI	5.37	3.22	6.18	3.34	2.52	2.09
	SULI	3.36	2.45	3.16	5.79	5.79	6.19
	SUBF	5.31	1.63	4.46	5.12	5.22	3.09

Market Research Studies – Multidimensional Scaling

MULTIDIMENSIONAL SCALING - SONITE MARKET

MULTIDIMENSIONAL SCALING - IDEAL VALUES (-20 TO +20)

Segment	Economy	Performance	Convenience
Buffs	-5.8	10.5	5.3
Singles	8.7	6.2	3.1
Pros	-15.6	12.5	-4.4
HiEarners	-10.3	1.0	5.2
Others	13.0	-7.3	-3.3

MULTIDIMENSIONAL SCALING - BRAND PERCEPTIONS (-20 TO +20)

Firm	Brand	Economy	Performance	Convenience
A	SAMA	12.6	-8.6	-8.2
	SALT	6.5	2.9	-1.1
	SAND	-13.3	12.7	-8.9
E	SEMI	-14.9	12.4	-3.6
	SELF	-15.1	13.1	-7.3
	SEBU	-5.5	10.7	5.7
	SERT	-12.0	1.0	5.2
I	SIBI	9.0	5.2	6.1
	SIPE	12.9	-9.4	-1.9
	SICK	8.2	2.6	6.1
O	SOLD	-10.6	1.6	5.5
	SONO	-14.4	12.2	-4.4
	SODU	9.3	5.3	2.3
	SODE	-6.5	11.3	4.0
U	SUSI	12.7	-8.5	-7.4
	SULI	-14.6	12.0	-5.7
	SUBF	6.0	8.0	-12.6

MULTIDIMENSIONAL SCALING
INFLUENCE OF PRODUCT CHARACTERISTICS ON MDS DIMENSIONS

	Weight (Kg)	Design (Index)	Volume (Dm3)	Max Freq (KHz)	Power (W)	Price ($)
Economy	Moderate	Slight	Slight	Slight	Slight	Very strong
Performance	Slight	Slight	Slight	Strong	Very strong	Slight
Convenience	Moderate	Moderate	Moderate	Slight	Slight	Slight

Market Research Studies – Perceptual map

MULTIDIMENSIONAL SCALING - PERCEPTUAL MAP
ECONOMY X PERFORMANCE

Horizontal axis :   Economy   (perceived economy, increasing from left to right)

Vertical axis :   Performance   (perceived performance, increasing from bottom to top)

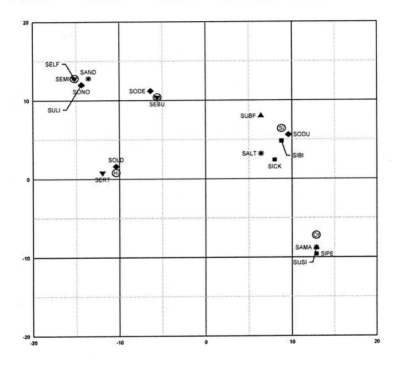

Market Research Studies – Perceptual map (cont'd)

MULTIDIMENSIONAL SCALING - PERCEPTUAL MAP
ECONOMY X CONVENIENCE

Horizontal axis :   Economy   (perceived economy, increasing from left to right)

Vertical axis :   Convenience   (perceived convenience, increasing from bottom to top)

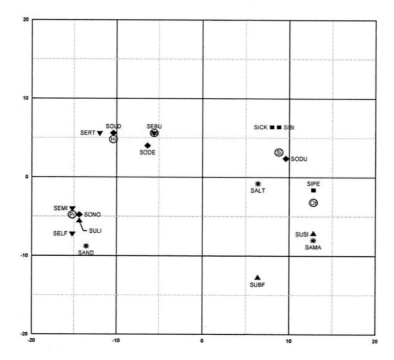

Market Research Studies – Market forecast

MARKET FORECAST - SONITE MARKET

MARKET FORECAST - SEGMENT SIZES AND GROWTH RATES

Segment	Buffs	Singles	Pros	HiEarners	Others	Total
Segment sizes in KU						
Actual size this period	133	614	265	245	708	1 965
Forecasted size next period	122	658	243	237	794	2 054
Forecasted size in five periods	87	865	173	209	1 258	2 592
Relative segment sizes in %						
Actual size this period	6.8%	31.2%	13.5%	12.5%	36.0%	100.0%
Forecasted size next period	6.0%	32.0%	11.8%	11.6%	38.6%	100.0%
Forecasted size in five periods	3.4%	33.4%	6.7%	8.1%	48.5%	100.0%
Forecasted growth rates in %						
Next period	-8.2%	7.1%	-8.2%	-3.1%	12.2%	4.6%
Total over next five periods	-34.8%	40.9%	-34.8%	-14.6%	77.8%	31.9%
Average over next five periods	-8.2%	7.1%	-8.2%	-3.1%	12.2%	5.7%

Market Research Studies – Competitive advertising

COMPETITIVE ADVERTISING - SONITE MARKET

COMPETITIVE ADVERTISING - ESTIMATED TOTAL EXPENDITURES
(all numbers in K$)

Firm	Brand	Buffs	Singles	Pros	HiEarners	Others	Total
A	SAMA	150	150	150	150	1 000	1 600
	SALT	0	50	0	0	0	50
	SAND	0	0	50	0	0	50
	TOTAL	150	200	200	150	1 000	1 700
E	SEMI	300	300	2 000	300	300	3 200
	SELF	0	0	0	0	0	0
	SEBU	1 400	200	200	200	200	2 200
	SERT	250	250	250	1 650	250	2 650
	TOTAL	1 950	750	2 450	2 150	750	8 050
I	SIBI	200	1 350	200	200	200	2 150
	SIPE	150	150	150	150	1 250	1 850
	SICK	0	50	0	0	0	50
	TOTAL	350	1 550	350	350	1 450	4 050
O	SOLD	200	200	200	1 450	200	2 250
	SONO	150	150	1 100	150	150	1 700
	SODU	200	1 500	200	200	200	2 300
	SODE	900	150	150	150	150	1 500
	TOTAL	1 450	2 000	1 650	1 950	700	7 750
U	SUSI	200	200	200	200	1 400	2 200
	SULI	200	200	1 400	200	200	2 200
	SUBF	200	1 400	200	200	200	2 200
	TOTAL	600	1 800	1 800	600	1 800	6 600
TOTAL		4 500	8 300	6 450	5 200	5 700	28 150
AVERAGE BY BRAND		265	371	379	306	335	1 656
AVERAGE BY FIRM		900	1 260	1 290	1 040	1 140	5 630

Market Research Studies – Competitive sales force

COMPETITIVE SALES FORCE - SONITE MARKET

COMPETITIVE SALES FORCES - ESTIMATED SIZES
(in number of salespeople)

Firm	Brand	Specialty stores	Depart. stores	Mass Merchandis.	Total
A	SAMA	28	33	34	95
	SALT	0	0	0	0
	SAND	0	0	0	0
	TOTAL	28	33	34	95
E	SEMI	32	20	22	75
	SELF	0	0	0	0
	SEBU	25	9	7	41
	SERT	18	31	13	62
	TOTAL	75	60	42	178
I	SIBI	12	13	10	35
	SIPE	9	20	27	55
	SICK	3	3	2	8
	TOTAL	24	35	40	99
O	SOLD	16	38	19	73
	SONO	20	11	10	41
	SODU	16	12	10	39
	SODE	10	4	2	16
	TOTAL	63	65	41	169
U	SUSI	5	21	42	68
	SULI	25	13	11	48
	SUBF	6	10	7	23
	TOTAL	36	44	60	139
TOTAL		226	238	217	680
AVERAGE BY BRAND		13	14	13	40
AVERAGE BY FIRM		45	48	43	136

Market Research Studies –Experiment

ADVERTISING EXPERIMENT - SONITE MARKET

EXPECTED RESULTS WITH INCREASED ADVERTISING BUDGET

	SOLD	SONO	SODU	SODE
Change in awareness (%)				
Buffs	0.5%	0.4%	0.8%	1.8%
Singles	0.2%	0.1%	1.1%	0.1%
Professionals	0.4%	1.0%	0.7%	0.4%
High earners	0.9%	0.3%	0.6%	0.4%
Others	0.2%	0.2%	0.2%	0.1%
Change in market share (%)				
Buffs	0.0%	0.0%	0.0%	1.9%
Singles	0.0%	0.0%	0.1%	0.0%
Professionals	0.0%	0.5%	0.0%	0.0%
High earners	-0.8%	0.0%	0.0%	0.1%
Others	0.0%	0.0%	0.0%	0.0%
Change in contribution after marketing (K$)	-459	42	-466	-127

Notes.

These results would have been achieved by a given brand if its advertising budget had been increased by 20% and if competitive actions had remained unchanged.

SALES FORCE EXPERIMENT - SONITE MARKET

EXPECTED RESULTS WITH INCREASED SALES FORCE

	SOLD	SONO	SODU	SODE
Change in number of distributors (U)				
Specialty stores	322	291	333	330
Depart. stores	41	80	85	45
Mass Merchandis.	107	124	129	49
Change in market share (%)				
Specialty stores	0.0%	0.1%	0.0%	0.1%
Depart. stores	-0.1%	0.1%	0.1%	0.1%
Mass Merchandis.	0.0%	0.1%	0.1%	0.1%
Change in contribution after marketing (K$)	-261	414	-124	53

Notes.

These results would have been achieved if the number of salespeople had been increased by 10 in each channel and if competitive actions had remained unchanged.

Market Research Studies – Conjoint analysis (segment Buffs only)

CONJOINT ANALYSIS - SONITE MARKET

CONJOINT ANALYSIS - RELATIVE IMPORTANCE OF CHARACTERISTICS

Segment	Design	Max Freq	Power	Price	Total
Buffs	15.0%	2.3%	27.4%	55.3%	100.0%
Singles	4.5%	4.2%	43.1%	48.2%	100.0%
Pros	13.3%	3.8%	42.0%	40.9%	100.0%
HiEarners	4.8%	3.4%	32.1%	59.8%	100.0%
Others	7.2%	1.8%	42.9%	48.1%	100.0%

CONJOINT ANALYSIS - UTILITIES - SEGMENT BUFFS

		Unit	1	2	3	4	Importance
Design	Level	Index	6	7	8	9	15.0%
	Utility	[0,1]	0.12	0.38	0.39	0.35	
Max Freq	Level	KHz	26	34	42	50	2.3%
	Utility	[0,1]	0.33	0.32	0.28	0.31	
Power	Level	W	51	67	83	99	27.4%
	Utility	[0,1]	0.07	0.47	0.57	0.14	
Price	Level	$	302	388	474	560	55.3%
	Utility	[0,1]	0.00	1.00	0.18	0.06	

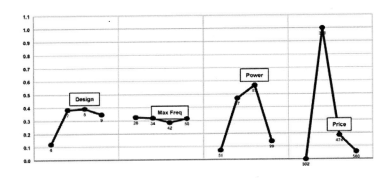

Blank Markstrat Online ID Card

MARKSTRAT
ONLINE by StratX

*Markstrat Online
ID Card*

REGISTRATION IS MANDATORY
Use the license number below to register on our website
www.markstratonline.com. Once registered you will be able to
obtain your username, password and download the software.

Use the back of this card to record your personal IDs.

www.markstratonline.com
www.stratx.com

STRATX
THE KEY TO STRATEGIC EXCELLENCE

Register on our
website to get your
personal username
and password.

Username

Password

Your instructor
will give you this
information which
you need to start
your Markstrat
Online course.

Course ID

Industry ID

Team ID

Team Password

INDEX